HARVEST

HARVEST

Collected Poems
and Prayers

by Ruth Firestone Brin

With an Introduction by
Charles E. Silberman

HOLY COW! PRESS • 1999 • DULUTH, MINNESOTA

Of the poems and prayers in this collection, copyright permission has been
obtained to reprint from the following, which first published these poems and
prayers:

THE RECONSTRUCTIONIST–*Celebration, Curacao, God of Men and Mountains,
The Ram, Simhat Torah, Through April,* and *Variation on an Ancient
Theme: the Kaddish.* IDENTITY–*For Nelly Sachs, Poem, the St. Croix River,
Saturday Morning in the Country of the Old Men: the Smoky Mountains
in October, Sun,* and *Winter.* THE JEWISH SPECTATOR–*The River, Miami Beach,
Genesis,* and *Created in the Image.* THE JEWISH FRONTIER–*Haluzim* and *Re-
turning to Jerusalem.* THE CCAR JOURNAL–*A Prayer for the Captives. Home
Movies* is reprinted from PRAIRIE SCHOONER by permission of the University of
Nebraska Press. Other writings first appeared in BITTERROOT, RECALL and JEW-
ISH HORIZON (Publication of the Religious Zionists of America).

Library of Congress Cataloging-in-Publication Data

Brin, Ruth Firestone.
        Harvest: Collected Poems & Prayers / Ruth F. Brin.–Rev., 2nd ed.
            p. cm.
        Includes index.
        ISBN 0-930100-89-1 (paperback)
        1. Jewish religious poetry, American. 2. Prayers. I. Title.
        PS3552.R4827H37   1999
        811'.54–dc21
                                                99-22745
                                                CIP

Publisher's Address:
Holy Cow! Press
Post Office Box 3170
Mount Royal Station
Duluth, Minnesota 55803

Holy Cow! Press books are distributed to the trade by Consortium Book Sales
& Distribution, 1045 Westgate Drive, Saint Paul, Minnesota 55114-1065.

This book is dedicated to my husband,
Howard B. Brin

Table of Contents

Section Three: *Barley*

Section Five: *Almonds and Raisins*

Introduction by
Charles E. Silberman

The problem of prayer, the late Abraham Joshua Herschel once remarked, is not prayer, but God. How much more so for many contemporary Jews, who have difficulty accepting the traditional conception of an all-powerful, all-knowing supernatural God embodied in Jewish liturgy!

Abandoning prayer is no solution. As Mordecai Kaplan pointed out more than a half-century ago, worship, particularly public worship, meets two fundamental human needs: the need to make life significant, and the need to identify oneself with a community—especially a community whose rituals and traditions provide that sense of significance. For Jews, prayer is not simply an encounter with God; it is a means of affirming one's membership in the Jewish people—of finding (and creating) significance by identifying oneself with that people and its historic mission.

Ruth F. Brin, whose meditations, prayers, and poems are collected here, is one of the liturgical pioneers of the post-World War II era. As early as the 1950s—the age of the "edifice complex," as it came to be called, when most American Jewish men seemed more concerned with the grandeur of the synagogues they erected than with the content of the prayers they uttered and most Jewish women seemed content with their traditional subordinate and passive role in public worship—Brin was trying to create a contemporary idiom for *kavanah* and struggling to reconcile traditional Jewish prayers and texts with modern sensibilities. As much as anyone, she was responsible for creating an atmosphere conducive to liturgical innovation and experimentation; it is hard to think of a new Reform, Conservative, or Reconstructionist prayerbook or anthology that has not included one or more of her prayers.

Given the traditional Jewish reverence for language, the question of the language of prayer is a large one. In the Biblical account of creation, it is through words that God brings the world into being; and in Jewish tradition, few offenses are more serious than *lashan ha-rah*, speaking ill of other people. Solving the problem of prayer, then, requires (among other things) finding an appropriate relationship between those who pray and the language they use.

That relationship does not require wholesale abandonment of the traditional liturgy; as Kaplan pointed out, "Only a philistine literalism can miss the poetic beauty and majesty" of many of the traditional prayers or the layers of meaning that centuries (in some cases, millennia) of repetition have added to them. To see the liturgy as fixed and unchanging, however, is to misunderstand—indeed, to distort—the traditional Jewish approach to prayer.

An understanding of that approach must begin with the dialectical nature of Judaism itself. The liturgy, in particular, is replete with dialectical tensions, e.g., between particularism and universalism; between the priestly and prophetic traditions; and between the centrality of Eretz Yisrael and the legitimacy and authenticity of the Diaspora. Part of the genius of the traditional Siddur is that it makes no attempt to resolve those tensions; the implicit message is not simply that the tensions themselves are crucial, but that each generation must try to resolve them in its own way.

In this instance, the most relevant dialectical tensions are those between *kevah*, the fixed order of prayer, and *kavanah*, the personal intent and concentration each individual brings to it; and between *kevah* and *ḥiddush*, or innovation. Historically, kavanah has implied *ḥiddush*; the siddur is filled with meditations and poems that represented an earlier generation's attempt to infuse inherited prayers with new meaning, but that became the next generation's *kevah*. Nothing could be more alien to the spirit of the siddur, in short, than the notion that "the new is forbidden."

The Reconstructionist Press is to be applauded for bringing Brin's collected works to the attention of the Jewish public; I hope they serve to encourage a new generation of men and women to follow her example. In the words of *Pirke Avot*, "it is not incumbent on you to finish the task; but neither are you free to desist from it."

Author's Preface

These poems and prayers were written over a period of time stretching from about 1950 to 1985. They are the harvest of most of my adult years, reflecting a personal search for the ultimate reality, the wonder, the mystery, the meaning that most of us call God. Many were written as liturgy, to share my search with other Jews through worship, but Harvest is more than a collection, since I have edited and revised many of the pieces.

Almost all of these poems and prayers have been published previously in books, magazines, prayerbooks and synagogue worship pamphlets. One group of readings interprets each of the weekly Torah portions; other poems are for different Jewish holy days, and many others simply grew out of my personal and religious life.

Although I make no claim to consistency, time has suggested some revisions. Others have been made to change "thee" and "thou" to "you" where possible, since new biblical translations, basic to contemporary worship, have made this change. Although I have considered myself a feminist all my life, I revised some language in the light of the new Jewish feminism and to express the feelings which I share with that group.

It is my hope that people who have read and recited my work in the past will find this new version even better; I greet new readers with the hope that they will find here true and meaningful writing.

My loving and beloved husband, Howard B. Brin, has been my greatest support in every way. My parents, Irma and Milton Firestone, encouraged me to write from my early childhood and gave me a deep feeling for the Jewish community. My children, Judith Brin Ingber, Aaron, David, and Deborah Brin, have each offered encouragement in special ways, Judith by choreographing some of my verse, Aaron by his thoughtful comments, David by setting my libretto to music, and Deborah by using my work in services she conducts as a rabbi.

Many rabbis, teachers, editors and friends have offered help in various ways; I can't list them all and have mentioned some in the introductions to various sections of the book. However, I want to thank Ira Eisenstein, David Teutsch, Stanley Rabinowitz, Bernard Raskas, Sidney Greenberg, Philip Goodman, Charles Davidson, Max Shapiro, Arnold Goodman, Barry Cytron, Trudy Weiss-Rosmarin, Meridel Le Seuer, Rhoda Lewin, and Mary K. Danos. I wish to express my indebtedness to those no longer living, whose memory is a blessing, Jerome Lipnick, Florence Lovell, Esther Rosenbloom, and Allen Tate. All of them and many others were of inestimable help.

Section One
Oranges and Olives

Sometime in the early fifties my family's rabbi, Stanley Rabinowitz, asked me to find poems he could use for responsive readings on Friday nights. It was a request which energized me and shaped my work for many years. What did I know about Jewish liturgy, prayer, Torah? He was willing to help, to start me on a long journey of study, writing, teaching.

Readings for a congregation require the imagery of poetry, a rhythm that is easy to speak, and comprehensibility. Private imagery is useless; this is public speech, which should be accessible to all of the congregation and should add meaning and emotional depth to the services.

My prayer-poems were frequently reproduced in the weekly "Order of Worship," and after a while, along with some of my more personal poems, they became my first book, *A Time to Search*, which was published in 1959. The next project was to write an interpretation for every sidra of the Torah designed to be read weekly in the synagogue. This became *Interpretations for the Weekly Torah*

Reading, published in 1965, the source of the second section of this book. I continued to write liturgy, which was used in many synagogues as well as the prayerbooks of all the major liberal groups—Conservative, Reform and Reconstructionist. "Oranges and Olives" will give readers a sample of my work.

God of Rain and Wind

God of rain and wind, of growth and destruction,
God of thunder and storm, of creation and decay,

I pray to You for myself, for well I know
That when a person dies a world is destroyed.

Every day that You continue me in life
You create my world afresh.

Make my soul pure as it came from You
And strengthen it for storm and wind.

Let me grow; destroy me, when the time comes,
Quickly, as You have done for others;

Give me, for a little while, a name,
That I may invoke Your name,
You terrible and nameless Lord of destruction.

Give me, for a little while, a voice,
That I may pray to You,
You great and nameless Lord of creation.

In the name of humanity, in our own words
I pray to You for Your children:

Be swift to straighten our twisted souls,
Swift as the wind-driven clouds.

Let love strike into us as lightning
And healing like a shower in the sun;

Let justice spring up as grass after rain
And mercy sparkle like sunshine on the wet lawn.

God of rain and wind, of growth and destruction,
God of sun and storm-cloud, of creation and decay,

In Your infinite mercy and lovingkindness
Continue us in life, create our worlds afresh.

A Woman's Meditation

When men were children, they thought of God as a
    father;
When men were slaves, they thought of God as a
    master;
When men were subjects, they thought of God as a
    king.
But I am a woman, not a slave, not a subject,
not a child who longs for God as father or mother.

I might imagine God as teacher or friend, but those
    images,
like king, master, father or mother, are too small for
    me now.

God is the force of motion and light in the universe;
God is the strength of life on our planet;
God is the power moving us to do good;
God is the source of love springing up in us.
God is far beyond what we can comprehend.

Southern Journey

Before the wind shakes the bronze leaves from the oaks,
While the maple is aflame and the poplar is still gold,

Flocks of birds take to the flyways of the continent
Down the great river valleys and along the seacoasts.

They fly above the changing landscape of autumn
Toward the warm lands of cypress and orange grove.

Sometimes we long to fly with them, to escape,
To send our souls away on a southern journey.

Lord God, who gave warbler, mallard and wren
The strength to migrate, the sense to know the way,
Give us strength to survive the cold seasons of our lives.

Help us through study and thought and meditation
To find the direction we are to travel,
With the same sure sense You have given the flying birds.

Help us through prayer and ritual and Your appointed
  days
To return even from the strange journeys of the soul
That take us to far countries of pretended peace.

We thank You, Oh Lord, for making us part of earth,
To wonder at its creatures, to exult in all its beauty.

We give thanks to You for making us part of heaven,
To see beyond the changing beauties of this fair earth,
To praise You and bless You who are creator of all.

God of Men and Mountains

As we drove up to the motel in the dark, we were listening to Edward R. Murrow on the car radio. We stopped, but we didn't go in. His voice was so compelling, and he was talking about the beginning of the Korean War. But what we were hearing was that voice broadcasting from London, during the blitz and the bombing attacks, when my husband was stationed there in the U.S. army and I listened night after night, after coming home from work in Washington, D.C. More war? Bombs dropping on us this time? When the broadcast was finished, I walked into the motel and wrote this poem, almost as you read it here. It is one of the few that I have done very little to rewrite. It was born whole.

God of men and mountains,
Master of people and planets,
Creator of the universe:
I am afraid.

I am afraid of the angels
You have sent to wrestle with me:

The angel of success
Who carries a two-edged sword,

The angels of darkness
Whose names I do not know,

The angel of death
For whom I have no answer.

I am afraid of the touch
Of Your great hand on my feeble heart.

Yet must I turn to You and praise You
Awful and great though You are
For there is none else.

There is no strength nor courage
But in You.
There is no life, no light, no joy
But in You.

Ḥaluẓim *

They came to this dried-up old woman of a land
Because they remembered she was once their mother.
Her lakes were salt as tears,
Her rocks protruded like ancient bones.
But they sweetened her waters and clothed her with green,
And she became fruitful as a young woman.
Israel, you are like Sara
Greeting the wonderful birth of Isaac
With toothless laughter.

*Pioneers in Israel

For My Father: Home Movies

My son, in color, swims prodigiously
leaps from pool feet first to diving board;
Skis, seconds later, backwards up the hill,
pulled by his flying scarf.

                      Another reel,
And I am child again. There's Dad
in bathing suit, straw hat, and pipe,
leading our horse toward the lake.
She pulls her head back, stretches her neck,
sets her hoofs apart on the sand. I forgot
how tall she was, but I remember
how my father walked, bow-legged, sturdy
on his feet, his elbows bent a little,
as though they too were bowed.
He grins at the camera, waves his pipe,
then takes the horse's bit to lead her,
knee deep, into water.

                      Our place
was sold. The horse died long before.
Never again in jest or pride will my father
walk before a camera.

                    Moving shadows
on a screen hold me here, resistant as the horse,
and take me by the bit (my mouth is soft)
and stretch my neck, and pull me deep
into the dark lake of memory.

Parents' Prayer

You who have planted in the brain of every spider
Foresight to provide food for the child she will never see;

You who have taught every sparrow enough wisdom
To push her fledglings from the nest;

You who have created the wasp an engineer
To build a house of paper for her child;

You who make of the brown bear a patient pedagogue
To feed and teach her unruly cubs;

Teach me, too, wisdom and foresight, skill and patience
Not to use instinctively, but with intelligence;

Help me to learn what I must know to raise these,
The most beloved and delicate of all Your creatures,
 my children.

"Created in the Image"

I pray Him bring me to repentance,
but I bring myself to sorrow
and the wish for death.

> I pray Him grant me forgiveness,
> but I grant myself pity
> and the sweetness of despair.

I lie in darkness
searching out the shape of my shadow,
and the night wind blows across my face.

> I know there is God,
> but who can touch a shadow,
> and who can find the wind?

I lie in darkness, praying,
and the shadow covers me,
and the wind cools me.

> Then I, who cannot touch, am touched;
> and I, who cannot form, am formed;
> and I, who cannot find, am found.

The Tree Trimmer

Dangling from a leather sling in the oak,
the tree trimmer, high in the swaying tree,
reaches out to saw away a branch.
It leaves a staring eye when it drops,
a round white eye on the tree trunk.
Cautiously, with rope and saw,
tools swinging from his belt,
he crawls upward, seeking limbs to cut.

Now I too slash away unnecessary branches,
opening eyes to the sky.
Imperiled, dangling, lacking skill to choose
the limbs that stifle growth, I pray
to You Whose marks I bear within
like rings of trees.
I pray You guide my hand,
I, the tree trimmer, I the tree.

September

Autumn will come. How shall I celebrate this solemn term?
I think: according to the custom of the worm.
Ignorant of wings and flight, I, too,
crawl upward to some unscaled height
and wrapped in silk secretions there, not knowing
whether bright wings, all cramped and hid, are growing;
whether I'll live, emerge and change, or if I'll die,
like an old leaf next spring, crumbling and dry;
I'll wait, like that green caterpillar there
wrapped tight in threads of self-secreted prayer.

A Sense of Your Presence

Among our many appetites
There is a craving after God.

Among our many attributes
There is a talent for worshiping God.

Jews who wandered in deserts beneath the stars
Knew their hearts were hungry for God.

Jews who studied in candle-lit ghetto rooms
Thirsted longingly after God.

In tent or hut or slum
Jewish women prayed to God.

But we who are smothered with comfort
Sometimes forget to listen.

Help us, O Lord, to recognize our need,
To hear the yearning whisper of our hearts.

Help us to seek the silence of the desert
And the thoughtfulness of the house of study.

Bless us, like our ancestors in ancient days
With that most precious gift: a sense of Your presence.

Brush us with the wind of the wings of Your being.
Fill us with the awe of Your holiness.
We, too, will praise, glorify, and exalt Your name.

During Amidah
in a Crowded Synagogue

Though I close my eyes
My shoulder touches my husband's arm
And I feel about me the people of the congregation
Turning the leaves of the prayer books,
Whispering the ancient words.

I try to think of You.
You are not close to me as this man;
You are not many as this congregation;
You are not small as this place of worship,
And You have no history like this people.
I have thought well enough what You are not
But nothing at all of what You are.

I open my eyes and see the golden letters *Anokhi Adonai*[1]
And below them *Lo* and many times *Lo*[2]
And I perceive that You have written what we are not to be
But not what we are, giving us this freedom,
Though having life we are not free of growth and change.
As they sway a little and read the words
The people pray that You bless what they are becoming.

The soul of my husband is sometimes very distant
Even though he stands so close and dear beside me;
You are distant, dwelling in the uttermost parts
Of the sea or far above the morning star,
And yet You are sometimes closer to me than my own
   breath.

Oh, You great and distant God
Send down Your holiness that we may love one another;

[1] "I am the Lord," beginning of Ten Commandments
[2] "No"—"Thou shalt nots"

Oh, You near and beloved God
Let my soul grow closer to You;

Oh, You dear and distant God
Accept my prayer and the prayers of all people.

Variation on the Kaddish

This is the hall, this the hush, this the hour
I rise to praise the Lord of all the living
and the lonely dead.

> I rise to praise:
> I raise my voice
> I lift my head
> Despite the sick
> Despite the dead
> Despite the cries
> of pain, I rise
> to praise my God.

> I praise the God
> Whom all folk praise
> with separate song,
> Who made the earth,
> the sky, the throng
> of those who raise
> in prayerful phrase
> their souls to Him.

This holy hour, this hush, this lull
I yield to Him whose glory is beyond all praise
and bless His name
and say Amen.

Section Two: Wheat
Falling in Love with The Book
(A Reading for each Sidra)

By a lucky chance during my junior year at Vassar College, I signed up for the Bible seminar. The professor, Florence Lovell, had been a missionary in China, where her four children were born; afterwards she earned a PhD from Oberlin College. She had travelled to Palestine before our class met. She was small, demanding, precise and a wickedly funny mimic. She was the most inspiring teacher I had in college, and she taught me to love the Bible and to love the people who had created it. She was able to combine an intellectual, scholarly approach with a deep respect for the Jewish people and a lasting love for their Book. There is no end to the study of the Bible, and since her introduction I have sampled many approaches. My poems can be only a dim reflection of the magnificence of the Torah, yet I have a lover's quarrel with the Book; I agonize over the long descriptions of animal sacrifice, the tedious descriptions of tabernacle building and the weird juxtapositions of the highest ethical principles with a prescription for curing a person or a house of leprosy. No matter, there is always something new to notice, to wonder about, to imagine and think about in that collection of books so densely packed with human experience and the search for God.

Creation

GENESIS 1, 2

When the divine word ended chaos and nothingness,
when God rolled away the darkness from the light,
that was the first moment of creation.

When Adam opened his eyes and beheld earth and heaven,
that was a moment of creation as real as the first,

For the sun is not bright without an eye to see,
the waves of the sea cannot crash and roar
without an ear to listen,

And unless life marks off the segments,
time is a dimension without measure.

Though we are finite,
God created us both free and conscious,
able to share in the power of creation.

Every moment that we behold anew the work of God,
the jewels of dew on morning grass,
the smile lighting the face of a beloved child,

Every moment that we work for good,
is a moment of creation.

Lord God, renew in us, in every one,
the bright mornings of Adam and Eve.

Let each dawn rise fresh with hope
as it was in the beginning.

Inspire us to create what is good;
quicken our delight in all that You create.

Genesis

GENESIS 1, 2

In the beginning, You made a simple world,
day and night, water and earth, plants and animals.

But now You create galaxies beyond systems
in the unending curve of space.

Now we know You create with subtlety
the invisible atom with its secret heart of power.

You create with delicacy, with violence,
the cell, splitting, becoming life.

Filled with joy, You make a human being,
a whole world, mysterious, delicate, violent.

Overflowing with joy, You create myriads of people,
fling galaxies across space, sow them with countless
   kinds of life.

Your love, massive, cosmic, joyful, explodes around us,
as in the beginning, in a burst of light, a rush of waters,
in the cry of birth, in ourselves, even in ourselves.

In Praise

GENESIS 1, 2

Hail the hand that scattered space with stars,
Wrapped whirling world in bright blue blanket, air,
Made worlds within worlds, elements in earth,
Souls within skins, every one a teeming universe,
Every tree a system of semantics, and pushed
Beyond probability to place consciousness
On this cooling crust of burning rock.

Oh praise that hand, mind, heart, soul, power or force
That so inclosed, separated, limited planets, trees, humans
Yet breaks all bounds and borders
To lavish on us light, love, life
This trembling glory.

Noah

GENESIS 6:9-10

When the sun rises and the night falls,
when spring follows close on the heels of winter,

Let us remember God's promise
that the rhythms of earth will uphold life forever.

When we sail, like Noah, on uncertain seas,
in a wooden boat no bigger than a toy;

When we fear, like Noah, that the end may come,
if not to all life, then to us,

When we look for small signs of hope,
a green leaf, or the branch of an olive-tree,

Let us remember the bow that spans the retreating
rain-clouds, and the promises God still keeps for us,
that seed-time and harvest shall not cease.

Then we can give thanks to God
for the fruitful earth, our dwelling place,
for God's blessings, bright as the rainbow
in the shining sky.

Abraham Goes Forth

GENESIS 12, 13, 15

Abraham left the city of his father
because the Lord sent him wandering.

He lived with his people in the desert,
moving from place to place to feed his cattle.

He saw how a puff of dust rises
with each step of a plodding camel.

He saw whirlwinds of countless dust particles
rise and spin in the shimmering heat.

At night when he left his tent, he saw
myriads of stars, flung like jewels across the sky.

The soul of Abraham was strong,
permitting him to question God,

The mind of Abraham stretched out,
reading promise in the stars and meaning in the dust.

Grant us, Lord of Abraham, moments to talk
beneath the stars, in town or wood or wilderness.

Let our souls be strong as Abraham's,
to contend with You, Lord our God,

Let our minds reach out, as the mind of Abraham,
toward the infinite promise of goodness in Your world.

To Be Repeated by the Seed of Abraham

GENESIS 22:17

I will bestow My blessing upon you and make your descendants as numerous as the stars of heaven and the sands of the seashore.

By what shore did Abraham walk
When he heard God's promise of posterity?

It must have been a broad and sandy beach
With stars flung like jewels across the sky.

Surely to number the grains of sand
Would have baffled the brain of Abraham;

Nor was he an astronomer
Who could count the stars,

Yet when he walked by the sea that night
His mind could leap to infinity.

Grant us, Lord, peace to walk beneath the stars
By field, or wood, or restless sea.

Let our minds dwell, as Abraham's did,
Not on known and numbered things but on You.

Let our souls reach out, as the soul of Abraham,
Rejecting zero, and with faith and vision, embracing infinity.

The Binding of Isaac

GENESIS 22

God spoke to Abraham, and Abraham said, "Here am I."

Isaac spoke to Abraham, and he answered, "Here am I,
my son."

The angel of the Lord called to him out of heaven,
and Abraham said, "Here am I."

For many things we honor our father, Abraham:

That he destroyed the idols of Terah
and set forth to find the living God;

That he found the Lord, our God,
and that he made with Him the first covenant;

Let us also honor him for this:
that he hid himself neither from God
nor from anyone who called;

That when his son spoke he answered with compassion,
that when God and the angels of God called,
he answered them with courage and faith.

From the voices that call to us,
The voices within and the voices of others,
let us not seek to escape.

God of our ancestors, help us to listen
in the spirit of Abraham.

Help us, when we are called,
to speak the words of Abraham: "Here am I" *

*Heb. "Hineni"

Abraham and Isaac

GENESIS 22

Abraham:
>I dreamed that my first-born of Sara
>would be the father of a great nation,
>a nation as numerous as the sands of the sea,
>as bright as the stars of heaven.
>I taught him to be a chieftain
>but I forgot that God demands of us our first-born.
>It is easier when they are infants,
>but now I know the lad, slender and quick;
>he leans against me and my hand rests on his
>   curly head.
>How can I do what I must do?
>Oh my God! I would give back every promise You
>   have made me
>for the life of my son, my only son, Isaac!

Isaac:
>My father led me up the mountain,
>tied me down on the uneven faggots
>with my head thrown back.
>I saw his hand, the knuckles white,
>clutching the knife with the jagged edge;
>I knew that when my throat was cut
>and my blood running out on the ground
>death might not come before the burning.
>But then my father's hand stopped in mid-air,
>and I heard the angry bleating of the ram.

Abraham:
>Oh God, I know You now,
>not as a maker of covenants,
>but as the giver of life.
>I pray to You:

Let my son dream his own dreams, not mine.
Let him make his own promises to You.
Let him live the life You have bestowed upon him
as You and he see fit.

Isaac:

My father used to teach me many things
so I could learn to be a great chieftain,
but since we went up on the mountain
he is quiet and gentle and only tells me
that as I grow older I, too, will speak with God.
When I wander in the fields at eventide
and sometimes watch a caravan pass by,
I think about my father finding the ram
and I wonder what God will require of me.

The Ram

GENESIS 22:13

You were hiding.
I left the others to look in the mountains,
picking my way upward all night
along the running streams.
Toward morning I thought I saw firelight
and stopped in thick underbrush.
Before me is a clearing, the mountain top.
A boy lies there on a pile of wood, bound with ropes.
Crouched over him is a man holding a flint knife.
They are frozen with foreboding.
When I try to run, branches crack.
How did my head get caught?
The man turns to me now, is coming
knife in hand, head lowered.
I cannot speak to people.
Oh where are You?
He comes and in his eye
is the cold glint of murder.

The Life of Sarah

GENESIS 24

We have heard, as our ancestors heard,
how Rebekah drew water from the well,
how Isaac lingered in the field at twilight.

When we hear the chanting of this story
we listen to the dimension of time
that is forever Israel's.

Sometimes when we lie awake at night
we hear the trains rumbling by,
the cars passing, the airplanes overhead.

We are listening to the vastness and distance,
the dimension of space that is America's.

Twice blessed are we, O Lord our God,
who may seek the freedom of space
and the wisdom of time.

Twice blessed are we, O Lord our God,
and render thanks to You
that we can hear the chanting of Israel,
and the night-sounds of America.

תולדות

TOLEDOT

The Generations of Isaac

GENESIS 27

It is written that Isaac loved Esau because
he brought meat,
but Rebekah loved Jacob, and for the mother's
love no reason is given.

To Jacob, who had his mother's love, his father's
blessing was given,
but from Esau, who had not his mother's love,
his birthright was taken away.

Jacob became at last a father of his people,
but not until he had run away in fear
and dreamed his dream,

Not until he wrestled with his angel and labored
twice seven years for the wife he loved,
for he who had deceived his blind father
was himself deceived.

Now while we have a measure of strength and
vision, Lord,
let us consider the birthright of our children.

Grant us wisdom to favor no child, and to be
deceived by no child,
Grant that we never weep the tears of Rebekah,
who had to send away her dearest son,

Grant that we never love a child for the gift
he brings,
lest we tremble with the tremblings of Isaac.

Help us give all our children their mothers' love
and their fathers' blessings from the beginning;
Help us give all our children their share
in the heritage of our people.

Jacob's Dream

GENESIS 28

The angels going up and down on the golden ladder
did not change Jacob's destination,
nor did the promises of God establish his manhood.

But after many years, when he had won Rachel,
when he was a bearded man, master of tents and flocks,
it is written that Jacob dreamed again.

This time he called together his family
to go to meet the brother whom he had wronged,
to turn again to the land and to the God of his fathers.

Maturity may come with work, and wisdom with years,
but let us always remember the dream and the vision
that are the gifts of God.

Let us remember how our ancestor, Jacob,
in the years of his maturity, left the place of his success
to return to the country and the ideals of his youth.

We pray that the glitter of all the wealth
we have worked to possess
will not blind our eyes to our own inner vision.

We pray for dreams in the years of our strength,
and for strength in the days of our dreams.

Jacob Becomes Israel

GENESIS 32, 33

Who can say whether Jacob wrestled with man or angel,
with his own fear and guilt, or with God?

I cannot answer, yet I know there is a spirit waiting
in the darkness to wrestle with me, and after we meet,
I shall never be the same.

Who can say how Jacob prevailed, in the darkness by the
river
against this fearful antagonist?

I cannot answer, yet I am sure there is a river on my way,
and when I cross it, I cannot return again.

Who can say whether Jacob was worthy of the mercies
that carried him to the wrestling and the river?

Whatever the worthiness of Jacob, surely I cannot
pray for help, except to the God of mercy and truth,
the God of Jacob.

It is to You we pray: let all who wait alone in darkness,
knowing their fear and their guilt, be to You as Jacob,

Let them be strong with the strength of Jacob's faith,
let them have Jacob's humility, and his courage,

Let them find, when they cross their rivers,
the glad peace that Jacob found.

Jacob

GENESIS 32:8-33

I sent my family on across the river,
Lovingly I helped them prepare their tents.

Tenderly I kissed my children and blessed them,
Not knowing if I would see them again.

Across the river from all I loved I waited alone,
Remembering the loneliness of God.

I sat by the moving waters in the darkness,
Waiting, listening, searching, yearning.

When He came I didn't know him,
Thinking He was another man.

But He seized me with violence
And I fought, panted, gritted my teeth.

Straining and twisting every muscle,
I struggled for my life, and my strength held.

In the morning He marked my thigh and changed my name
And sent me back across the river to my life.

Around the fires at night I tell my children this story,
Knowing that they will also search and struggle in the night.

In the darkness of my tent I pray to God
To remember my children, and to come to them.

I pray to God that through their struggles
They, too, will learn to know Him.

Joseph

GENESIS 37

Joseph strutted before his brothers wearing
his gaily colored coat, the garment of a prince,
and the sign of his father's favor.

Yet three times would Joseph go down into the pit:
the dry well where his brothers threw him,
the abyss of slavery, and the black hole of prison.

Three times Joseph would know suffering,
despair, and his own helplessness,
and three times he would call to God from the depths.

Only after he had understood himself,
only after he had served faithfully and well,
only after he had pondered the dreams of others,
were his own dreams fulfilled.

When he met his brothers again,
he was no vain lad, but a ruler of Egypt,
reaching toward them with compassion.

Oh Lord of all generations, You know the human soul.
From pits dug for us by enemies and friends
and by ourselves, we cry out to You.

We pray to grow as Joseph grew,
from vanity to kindness, from folly to wisdom,
from childishness to maturity.

Oh keep us from praying for favors we have not earned,
or for the bright garments of easy privilege.

Send us hope when we go down to the inevitable pits.
Send us Your help when we recognize our helplessness.

Joseph and Pharaoh

GENESIS 41

The nakedness of Joseph before Pharaoh
was the nakedness of an elm tree in the winter.

Not like the pine, whose branches hold the snow,
and bend and break in the cold, stood Joseph,

But like the elm, stripped of his colored garments,
the ornaments of his youthful summer,
stripped of his pride as favorite son,
of his pretensions to rule his brothers,

Yet rooted in the teachings of his fathers,
as the elm tree is rooted in the even temperature
of the deep earth,
Joseph stood before the king of Egypt.

The fine branches of his intellect
and the myriad fibers of his nerves
were exposed to the chilling air of the court.

The nakedness of Joseph before the Pharaoh
was a nakedness which both exposes and protects.

It is the nakedness of Jacob before the Wrestler—
for Jacob had sent his wealth, his family,
his pretensions and his pride, across the river.

It is the nakedness of Moses before God—
for Moses had left behind him the power
and the privilege of a prince in Egypt.

It is the nakedness of the Jew in history—
the nakedness of honesty and humility,
of innocence and abnegation, of deep roots and bare
branches,
of protection and exposure.

It is a nakedness neither to escape nor embrace,
but to accept, if it comes, as we have done
in every age.

Joseph and His Brothers

GENESIS 45

Joseph had learned to rule,
to please Pharaoh, to command slaves;

He moved quietly among the priests and princes
thinking he pulled the strings of these puppets
so gently they thought they moved themselves.

Now that the rude shepherds from Canaan
stood before him, he considered carefully
how to make them bring down Jacob and Benjamin.

He looked at his brothers; what were they to him
but the ones who sold him into slavery?

They were sheaves meant to bow down to his sheaf,
stars meant to bow down to him.

What were these tired wanderers
to the lord of Egypt?

Only the means for him to gain news
of his beloved father and brother.

Yet when he spoke roughly to them
he had to turn away and weep.

This was the heart of Joseph,
that he had to weep in spite of himself.

This was the greatness of Joseph,
that he was unable to use his brothers
as tools in his hands.

Remember Joseph when you plan to use a person
as a tool, and weep instead.

Remember Joseph when you seek dominion
over others, like sheaves or stars,
and weep instead.

Pray God that you remember Joseph well.
Pray God let every person be to you
like a lost brother.

The Death of Jacob

GENESIS 49

As Jacob lay dying
he had strength to bless his sons
and time to speak his prophecies.

But in our time
death is a hungry hunter
pursuing us on the highway,
overtaking us in the fastest planes;

Dying, there may be for us no long farewells,
no blessings, and no prophecies.

Living, then, we must bless our children,
placing our hands upon them
and turning their faces toward God;
living, we must struggle for a better day.

To foretell the future
may be a patriarch's privilege,
but to take the future in our hands is urgent
and to make it good shall be our human glory.

Oh God of Jacob, while yet we live,
help us to guide our children in love and wisdom,
help us now to build a world of peace.

The Burning Bush

EXODUS 3

It was no bush, but Moses' soul, touched
by the finger of God, that flamed and burned.

Perhaps in that ecstasy he wished for death
but he burned and was not destroyed,
he flared up, but was not consumed.

God sent him, against his will, to the slaves in Egypt.
God made him, with the fire of faith, a wise and mighty
leader.

For in the light of faith the mind understands,
in the warmth of faith the heart loves,
and in faith the soul finds its joy.

Of all Your blessings, God, faith is the first;
we beseech You, Lord of all peoples,

Touch us with Your fire,
burn us with Your flame,
with faith in You, make us whole.

Moses and Aaron

EXODUS 7

Sometimes we have dwelt on the sufferings
of our ancestors, Pharaoh's slaves,
on their broken backs and stunted spirits.

Yet think now of the people of Egypt,
who would endure ten plagues
because of the hard heart of their Pharaoh.

Jew or Egyptian, a first-born child is a baby,
and death is final.

In this century we specialize in self-made plagues:
fascism, fallout, and nuclear fission.

Our scientists are like the magicians of Egypt:
they can pollute the wells of life,
but cannot make them clean again.

Our plagues are efficient and impartial:
they fall on Egypt and Goshen,
on innocent and guilty, man and beast alike.

Will men and women and their leaders
ever become wise enough, and good enough,
to reduce our plagues to a flick of wine
on a white tablecloth?

The Last Plagues

EXODUS 10

After a crater erupts, volcanic ash may blacken
the sky and make the sunsets lurid for months;

There are eclipses of the sun, the stinging
darkness of dust storms, and the totality
of blackout.

All of these remind us of the Egyptian darkness,
so thick it could be tasted and felt.

Could the children of Israel, rebellious
and frightened slaves, have lit their homes
with the symbolic light of faith or good deeds?

Perhaps they cherished a glimmering hope
that they could achieve greatness on earth,
rather than in the pyramids of the dead.

Perhaps they blew on the spark of their hope
that Israel, the lowliest of peoples,
might achieve freedom.

In the thick darkness of the Egyptian night
they could not foresee how often the nations
would shoulder them out into the shadow,

How often their freedom would be reduced
to a flicker, burning for a moment
after the oil is gone.

We pray You renew this miracle for us:
that in the darkness of our age, in blackout
and rejection, in fear and ignorance,
You will cause a light to burn for us,

A light of learning, a light of freedom,
a light of faith, a light of good deeds.
These are the lights we pray will burn together
to make a bright blaze of hope for our world.

The Passage of the Sea of Reeds

EXODUS 15:1, 8, 10, 11

"Then Moses and the Israelites sang this song to the Lord.
They said:
I will sing to the Lord for He has triumphed
gloriously
Horse and driver He has hurled into the sea . . .

At the blast of Your nostrils the waters piled up,
the floods stood straight like a wall;
the deeps froze in the heart of the sea . . .

You made Your wind blow, the sea covered them;
They sank like lead in the majestic waters.

Who is like You O Lord among the celestials,
Who is like You majestic in holiness
Awesome in splendor, working wonders!"

Might we have gone backward into slavery,
had we chosen to forsake Moses?

Who is like You, Oh Lord,
Who has delivered our destiny into our own hands?

Of all the wonders You have wrought,
We praise Your name for this:

That You have created a world whose workings
we can probe with the marvelous tool of our minds,
and alter with the skillful work of our hands,

That You in your love
have given us the awesome gift
of freedom and responsibility to choose our own ways.

The Ten Commandments

EXODUS 18-20

And the words which were spoken to the people
from the fiery mountain were ten.

In Egypt the priests were powerful and rich
because they knew the secrets of the Book
of the Dead;

In Greece the oracles revealed the fates
determined by capricious gods for princes
or warriors;

In Babylon the priests taught each other
mysteries too deep for ordinary folks to fathom.

But in Israel there is no secret and privileged
priesthood, we are a holy people.

In Israel the heart of the mystery is the ten
commandments, so easy to understand a child
can recite them as he counts on his fingers.

In Israel we pray for God's help
when we make the difficult effort
to perform His commandments.

Strangers

EXODUS 22:20

You shall not wrong a stranger or oppress him,
for you were strangers in the land of Egypt.

We were strangers in Egypt and Kiev,
we were foreigners in Babylon and Berlin,

We were outsiders and wanderers
in Spain and Poland and France.

We looked at the citizens of those lands
with the dark pleading eyes of the alien.

Our hearts beat the hesitant beat
of those without rights, fearful and uncertain.

We pray You help us to remember
the heart of the stranger
when we walk in freedom,

Help us to be fair and upright
in all our dealings with other people.

O, burn and brand the lesson
off all the years and all the lands
on our hearts.

Lord, make us forever strangers
to discrimination and injustice.

How To Build the Tabernacle

EXODUS 25-27

What did they build first after they left Egypt?
they built the sanctuary.

God commanded them to begin the sanctuary with
the Ark
so that He could dwell among them.

According to the word of God, our ancestors built
the Ark,
and because their hearts were willing
they built themselves into the people
who could carry the Ark in their midst.

We pray to begin what we build in the presence
of God,
we pray to begin each day and each year
with the word of God;

We pray to begin each task and each hour
according to the will of God,
so that, like our ancestors, we may build
and become what is good.

Our God and God of our past and future,
in You alone is goodness and holiness.
Be with us in the thousand beginnings of our lives.

The Priest's Garments

EXODUS 28

The garments of the high priest were of such beauty,
the jewels so radiant, they dazzled the people.

Daily in the sanctuary he made sacrifices to the Lord,
sacrifices of the lamb and the bull,
the dove and the little cakes.
To the shepherds and farmers
who brought these sacrifices,
animals and grain were the means of life;

Thus they proclaimed their willingness
to give life itself to God.

In all ages, at all times
people have traded value for value:

Salt or sea-shells or gold
for the things they wanted,

But for those who love God
the only sufficient gift to give

Is the symbol of life
or life itself.

Will You accept as sufficient
our prayers and our attempts to pray
as You once accepted the lambs and grain
of our ancestors?

Will You accept our struggling efforts
to return love for hostility
and justice for partiality?
Will You find our study acceptable?

Teach us, Oh God, the spirit of sacrifice:
how to devote our lives to our highest ideals.

The Golden Calf

EXODUS 32

Aaron, the Levite, of Egypt,
was an accomplished magician.

He could turn a stick into a snake,
then grasp its tail and change it back to wood.

He could turn the waters of the Nile to blood;
he could touch the dust with his rod
and transform it into a swarm of gnats.

All this, it is written, he did
according to the instructions
Moses received from the Lord.

Like the Egyptians, Aaron could take golden rings
and bracelets, melt them in the fire, and make a god,

A golden calf that people could see
and touch and worship in the old ways:
with festival and frenzy.

All this Aaron could do,
and impressively.

Yet the wonders wrought by his brother, Moses,
have made us forget the skill of Aaron,

For Moses transformed a tribe of slaves
into a free people;
Moses discovered and proclaimed the laws of God.

In our deepest prayers we must ask for strength
to forsake the beguiling illusions of our day,
like the easy magic of Aaron.

We must ask for wisdom to accept
the challenge of Moses:

To learn to make changes through long
and patient leadership,
to discover and uphold the laws of righteousness
for our own times.

Attributes of God

EXODUS 34

Angry and afraid, unsure of himself, carrying the second
   set
of heavy stone tablets, Moses returned alone to Sinai.

As he took the familiar rocky path that wound, snakelike,
up the steep mountain, he looked down on the scattered
   tents of the children of Israel.

He saw the ugly scar on the earth where the golden calf
had been burned.
When he looked up, he saw the cloud,
waiting on the mountain top.

God might abandon Moses now and forget the sinful
   people in the camp below.
He might leave them to the scorching wilderness
or to the cruel tribes who waited at the edge of the desert.

"Abandoning us would be justice," Moses thought
as he struggled up the mountain, "divine justice."

As he approached the whirling, roaring cloud, a great wind
turned him and forced him into a cleft in the rock.

It held him there while a voice spoke: "Adonai, Adonai,
El rahum v'hanum . . ."

In the whirling vortex of power at the heart of his universe,
Moses discovered the voice of compassion and forgiveness,
the voice of his God, his ultimate truth.

It is good to try to be like Moses, a man who returned
to God, a man whose fear and anger left him
when he experienced divine mercy.

It is good to try to be like Moses, who was reborn
in the cleft of the rock, with renewed faith and strength
to lead his people out of the wilderness.

It is better, it is sublimely daring, to try to be
like the God of Moses, to act always with patience and
    mercy,
with love and kindness, grace and compassion, infinite care.

No Sheltering Place

EXODUS 33:18-23

The Lord gave Moses no sheltering place
but the cleft of the rock.

If I could refuse the protection
of thick walls

If I could free myself from my house
and everything in it

If I were willing to thirst by day
and shiver by night

If I could lie quietly watching the stars
through the branches

If I could listen to the night wind
shepherding the clouds

Then might my soul be open to You?
Then might I hear as my ancestors heard?

I gather harvest of the years they lived
exposed to rain and sun, open to You.

I gather strength and bravery from them
so I may bring You this harvest-offering:

This willingness to hear the voice
that cries from the depths of stillness

This willingness to try to hear,
as the winds and the stars hear,
in steadfast obedience to Your teachings.

They Build the Tabernacle

EXODUS 35, 36

To devotion God set no limits.
and to dedication of the spirit
God set no bounds;

But great quantities of tribute God did not demand,
and the people were restrained from bringing
too much gold for the Tabernacle.

Though the Temples of Solomon and Herod
were far more costly,
it is written that the Divine Presence was found
more constantly in the humbler structure.

To dedicate the spirit to God is more difficult
than to give money,
to devote the whole heart to the Lord
is more difficult than bringing gifts.

Not because of the gold on the walls
does the light of the sanctuary shine forth,
but because of the spirit within.

Those who worship carry away with them
more than they bring
for they find there the light to illumine
their lives.

The Tabernacle Completed

EXODUS 38

Babel was built to defy deity,
to declare the dominion of man;

Bricks were passed from hand to hand
for a whole year
to reach the masons at work on the top
of the tower.

Thus, they wept when a brick fell
but when a man toppled to his death,
they turned their backs.

The tower of Babel was built to glorify man,
but they achieved degradation and destruction.

The sanctuary was built in obedience to God,
in recognition of His dominion.

The tent proved to be far greater than the tower;
hangings of cloth outlasted brick and mortar.

In the ark built to the glory of God
we find our own essential glory:
righteousness and holiness
in the imitation of God.

The Book of Leviticus

LEVITICUS 1

The contemporary eye,
the cold and factual eye,
would not linger on this book,
seeing in it only an archaic account
of priests, slaughtering cattle,

But there is another way to read,
even in the twentieth century,
if you will remember
not the ritual, but the people,
not the priest, but the shepherd.

The shepherd stands in the courtyard
of the Temple, his feet dusty from his journey;
the soil cannot be removed
from the cracks in his hard hands;
he holds a ram by a rope around its neck.

When the robed priest approaches,
the shepherd puts his hand on the ram's head,
and as the priest takes his offering
and carries it to the altar,
he watches closely.

There are all the hours he has spent
in sun and cold, watching those sheep,
his hours of loneliness in the high pastures,
his hours of despair at midnight
when a ewe dropped a stillborn lamb.

In the priest's hands
is his best ram, unblemished,
the best days of his years,
and the priest takes this offering
and makes it holy.

59

Now as the sacrifice is completed
a great joy fills the shepherd's heart;
his eyes shine with it:
God has accepted him,
God has accepted his life and his work.

Priest and shepherd are gone now,
but we turn to the pages of the book, searching;
we also need to sanctify our lives,
but for this there are no instructions
in our books of the twentieth century.

O Lord our God, and God of our ancestors,
shepherd and priest and prophet,
help us to read this book,
teach us to translate its spirit
into the language of our lives.

Prophet and Priest

LEVITICUS 6-8

Moses, one hand on Aaron's shoulder,
the other on his great staff,
led his brother to the tabernacle;

Carefully he instructed him
in the duties of his office.

Prophet and priest they went together,
brothers who led their people.

Without a prophet, the priest might serve
a false god,
without the priest and the sons of the priest,
the prophet's teachings might be lost.

Moses had seen the awesome and sacred fire
of Sinai,
he taught his brother, Aaron, to keep a fire
burning continually before the altar.

Whether tended and tame, or wild and free,
fire transforms dead wood into heat and light;
fire changes a solid thing into flame,
leaping upward.

We who must be priests to ourselves,
who must tend the daily fires in our souls,
pray to You

Lord God of Moses and Aaron,
of prophet and priest,
let the fires we tend give warmth and light,
let the flames of our souls leap upward toward You.

The Priests Begin Their Work

LEVITICUS 10, 11

Though many of the ways of our fathers have been burned
away by time, we Jews are not consumed.

Though priest and Levite have burned away, holiness and
purity are not consumed, and the distinction between the
clean and the unclean remains.

The sin offering and the guilt offering have burned away
but justice is not consumed.

Though ark and Temple are turned to ashes, worship is
not consumed.

> Lord God, You hold in Your hand the twelve tribes,
> like the precious stones on the breastplate of the
> High Priest,
> You hold all the people of the earth,
> like a handful of jewels

Though we cannot penetrate the mysteries that are
in ourselves and beyond ourselves

Teach us for all time the unity of these: justice, purity,
holiness, and the worship of You.

תזריע
TAZRIA

Laws of Purification

LEVITICUS 13

Though it was difficult, long ago, to heal
the dread and deadly spots of leprosy,
it is also difficult to heal the deadly hatreds
we carry in our hearts today;

How shall we even recognize, beneath their bland
and persuasive smiles,
those who are diseased with corruption?

How can we banish the evil
that seeps into our own minds?

Oh Lord our God, we whose souls are blemished
and whose minds are impure, ask of You.

By what rites can we be clean again?
By what ceremony can we be cured of all our moral
illnesses?

Teach us, we implore You, as You taught Moses,
the ways of righteousness and strength.

Help us to heal ourselves and to be physicians
to those who need us

Make our souls pure, as they came from You.

Delight

LEVITICUS 14, 15

Long after the Temple was destroyed, and the sages
had substituted prayer for sacrifice,
the people remembered the rites of purification.

The mothers in the ghetto would wave the holiday bird
over the heads of their children, to atone for sin and evil.

We read, and we remember, and we wonder.

How shall we rise above the circumstances of our lives,
as the living bird rose over the open field?

How shall we find words for prayer as pure
as the trill of the wild bird singing?

Nature demands of the bird flight and song,
and how beautifully he sings in the branches,
how swiftly he flies the summer skies,

Oh Lord our God, may we do our tasks as well,
whether we are required to achieve or to pray,
to study or to sacrifice.

As we delight in the swoop and glide
and ascending arc of the flight of birds,
so may You find delight in us,
when we strive for our own human achievement.

Atonement in Spring

LEVITICUS 16

The earth turns, the seasons roll,
the days lengthen now to warmth and spring,
yet the passage prescribed for us to read this day
tells us to observe the Day of Atonement

The Torah speaks of Yom Kippur
while the trees bud joyously outside our windows.

Perhaps the Torah speaks now, in the spring,
of atonement, because we know so well
our songs of joy carry with them
the counterpoints of tragedy.

Studying the ancient ways
we shall seek atonement,
we shall seek unity with God,
whose holiness is beyond our logic and our imagination.

You Who are Lord of the deep rhythms of life,
of sun and rain, of sin and forgiveness,
You Who are Master of the ultimate mysteries:
of Your holiness, of our tragedy and of our joy,

We thank You, Lord,
now and in the season of our repentance,
that You have taught us atonement,
and offered us forgiveness.

Love Your Neighbor

LEVITICUS 19

In the center of the Torah is the Book of Leviticus,
in the middle of Leviticus is the chapter on holiness,

At the core of the chapter on holiness
is the command to love your neighbor as yourself.

You are in the midst of Israel,
trying to begin by loving your neighbors.

But before you can love your neighbor,
you must have achieved love of yourself.

Before you can revere your parents,
you must have struggled to fulfill the demands
of parenthood yourself.

Before you can love a stranger,
you must have been a stranger in a harsh land.

Lord, how can we possibly experience enough
and understand enough
to love as You love?

From the deep center of our beings, we pray:
Lead us toward wisdom and humility,
teach us compassion and understanding,

For we long to feel the holiness of Your presence
at the inmost center of our lives.

The Holy Days

LEVITICUS 21-24

The Lord has appointed a day of solemnity for us
in the fall, when we must drop our pretenses,
as the maples drop their scarlet leaves
into the rain pools;

God has chosen a day of remembrance for us in the spring,
when we must remember Egypt, as the returning robins
remember their nesting places,
as the splashing salmon their spawning grounds.

Knowing the unpredictable succession of sunshine
and turbulence in the human heart,
the Lord has appointed every seventh day
the season for thoughtfulness, the sabbath,
the day of rest.

But for the sanctification of the name of God,
there is no season, and for martyrdom
there is no appointed day.

In the best of times and in the cruelest of times,
others have demanded of us, and God has not denied us
the giving of our lives.

We pray that no days shall ever again be like the days
of German power and Roman empire;

We pray to be able to sanctify the name of God
in our lives, at His appointed seasons,
and not in our deaths.

בהר

BE-HAR

Testament of Freedom

LEVITICUS 25

The people of America read
about the sabbatical year
and the year of the jubilee
as a testament of freedom.

In the beginning they engraved
the words of Leviticus on the Liberty Bell:
"Proclaim liberty throughout the land
unto all the inhabitants thereof."

Generations later, the slaves,
in hopes of their freedom,
sang "The year of the Jubilo"
and "Go down, Moses."

You made us to be free;
You set the spark
in every human heart.

Now help us fan the spark to flame,
to light our way,
Now help us break the chains,
tear down the walls,

Help us bring freedom at last
to all the world.

Starlight: After Finishing the Book of Leviticus

LEVITICUS 26, 27

The words of our ancient tradition
come to us across thousands of human-years,

Like the starlight in early evening
that travels thousands of light-years
through space to come to us.

We cannot read by the glimmer of starlight,
and the star from which it came
may have exploded in a shower of meteorites
in an age long before we appeared on earth.

Moses disappeared on Mount Nebo,
and the bones of Abraham and Isaiah and the others
have long since disintegrated in the slow-motion
explosion of dust and decay.

We cannot read by this starlight,
clear and pure though it be,
yet sailors at sea have found their way home
by the stars.

Oh let the navigators of our people
remember the words of our tradition,
shining out like a pure point of starlight
in the gathering dusk.

In the Wilderness

NUMBERS 1-4

With the numbers of those who are here recounted,
our ancestors, God led us into the wilderness;

Divided the Red Sea for us;
Spoke to us from the fires of Sinai;
Revealed Himself to Moses
in a rushing wind.

Earth, water, fire, and air,
these are the elements of our existence.

God gave them to us on the day of creation,
gave them to us at the time of the Exodus,
gives them to us every day of our lives.

O praise God whose Law is His gift to every one,
as free as fire, as near as air,
as basic as water and earth,

O praise God, the rock and the ground of our being,
Who gives us the fires of faith,
the breath of spirit,
the still waters of peace.

The Silver Bowl and the Golden Spoon

NUMBERS 7

Here is the tale of Naḥshon, the young prince of Judah,
whose faith was very great.

Because he was the first to leap into the Red Sea,
he was appointed first prince
to bring his offering to the sanctuary.

In humility and faith he strode across the desert sands,
bearing high the silver platter.

Behind him came members of his family,
bringing the silver bowl and the golden spoon,
while driving before them the young animals
intended for the sacrifice.

It is a consequence of faith, be it reward or penalty,
that one who has faith leaps first into danger,
and one who has faith is the first to sacrifice
possessions and even self.

Today the silver vessels of the descendants of Naḥshon
are not empty, nor is the golden spoon exhausted.

Like Abraham and Rebekka and the young prince,
there are people in our day who have faith
and its consequent qualities—courage
and the ability to sacrifice.

We pray for them that they lead us
through the seas of despair
to the place of peace.

We pray for faith for ourselves,
knowingly accepting its consequences,
for with self-sacrifice comes true leadership
and with courage, humanity can leap forward.

From Sinai to Moab

NUMBERS 11:25

Then the Lord came down in a cloud and spoke to him;
He drew
upon the spirit that was on him and put it on the seventy
elders. And . . . they spoke in ecstasy (prophesied).

Moses felt no envy when God gave the gift of prophecy
to others,
for Moses sought what was good for his people.

He had led in battle, had decreed judgment,
had spoken with God,
yet Moses was truly humble.

With the eyes of eternity he looked down on us.
He had seen the loneliness of each individual
and the shortness of his life;

He had seen the weakness of human love
and the power of hatred and anger;

He had seen the goodness in men and women,
furled up as tight as the petals of a bud
that has not opened, and yields no fragrance.

Moses learned humility, because he saw himself,
a man like other men, frail and angry,
the flower of his dream unopened.

O Lord of Moses, we pray to see ourselves clearly,
to accept our human condition,
to find the humility whose source is wisdom.

Moses, Moses

NUMBERS 7-12

In your tent in the wilderness,
did you not long to lie again,
cradled in the princess' corruption,
satisfied with royal sweets,
a fondled foundling?
In her royal suite what manner of love
did she teach you, little brother in Egypt?
You left her couch for rocks and sand,
for vultures circling in the hot sun,
for some distant oasis where the gardens were not too lush,
nor the slaves too willing, nor the rulers too rich.
Egypt we know well,
and the wasteland is often our home,
but your Promised Land, Moses,
does anyone ever enter it?

From the painted glance of the princess,
her priestess' soul, stately and cruel,
From the forest of painted columns
and the statue of the god the sun could never reach,
From the woven and colored linen,
the barges floated down the Nile,
the quail roasted with garlic and leeks,
From the cunning craft and clever skills
that let us deed delicacies to the silent dead,
You, Moses! delivered us,
cursed us with conscience,
burdened us with identity,
blessed us with eyes that look from Nebo,
but left us with feet that have not entered.

An Assumption of Faith

NUMBERS 13, 14

This was the report of Caleb and Joshua:
that a band of nomad slaves could conquer a settled land,
that a people decimated by illness and warfare
could overcome fortified cities.

This was a minority report, for the ten spies
who went with them saw the enemy as giants,
and the land of Canaan invincible.

The people believed the ten,
and were afraid,
but Caleb and Joshua reasoned upon an assumption of faith.

In their experience is our history:
we are a people who continuously file a dissenting report
based on the assumption of faith.

In their lives is our hope,
for after forty years, Caleb and Joshua
entered the promised land.

Though we may stumble in the wilderness for
forty times forty generations,
Lord God of Israel, we pray:

Let the call of the silver trumpets that blew
when Caleb and Joshua entered the promised land
ring in our ears.

Let the silver trumpets of faith sound in our souls,
Sustain us, as You sustained our ancestors
in the wilderness.

The Rebellion of Koraḥ

NUMBERS 16, 17

Moses, in his extremity at the rebellion of Koraḥ,
asked God for a sign and a miracle.

The earth opened up and swallowed the rebels,
and fire consumed the followers of Koraḥ.

Yet though they were terrified,
the people continued to murmur against Moses and God.

After fire and plague and death did not avail,
God chose a new sign,
a small thing, a rod, a dead stick of almond wood
which overnight blossomed and bore fruit.

The complaining people accepted this sign
of the priestly rights of the house of Levi
and the divine appointment of Moses to lead them.

What did they think who were not convinced
by death and terror,
when they looked at the blossom and fruit
of that almond branch?

Perhaps they saw in it a sign and symbol
of God's greatest miracle,
the ever-present miracle of creation:

Perhaps they saw in it a reminder
of the ordered rhythm which God sustains in nature,
remembering how we depend on blossom-time
and bearing-time every day of our lives.

Perhaps when they saw the growing fruit,
they saw the potential for human growth,
God's miraculous gift to each one of us.

And Moses? Did he see that the miracles
which beget faith are not miracles of destruction,
but miracles of creation and of love?

Open our eyes, O God, to blossom and branch,
to all Your true and continuing miracles,
that we may perceive Your creation and Your love.

Purification

(SABBATH OF PURIFICATION, NUMBERS 19)

We are enjoined to study this ancient ceremony of
purification,
the ritual of the red heifer,
and to purify ourselves before the Passover.

How the ashes of a yearling cow could purify
we do not understand.

Water, we know, can wash us clean,
but is that purification?

In the fires of life, if we are lucky,
Cowardice and foolishness will melt down,
and we will draw out pure courage.

In the intense heat of our souls, can we forge
the worldly and the mysterious into the truly spiritual?

We pray for the dedication that can purify and subjugate
even our evil impulses.

We pray to achieve that purity of personality
that can turn every human element in us toward God.

The Waters of Meribah

NUMBERS 20:7, 8

*And the Lord spoke to Moses, saying, 'You and your
brother, Aaron, take the rod and assemble the community
and before their very eyes order the rock to yield its water.'*

Moses must provide water for his people
by obeying one more strange command of his God—
neither to dig a well nor to pray for rain—
but to speak to a rock.

Still mourning Miriam, taunted and angered
by the rebellious crowd,
his people must have seemed to him
as obdurate, as obstinate, as unmalleable
as the rock itself.

Yet when Moses struck the rock,
water came forth;
when he spoke to his rock-like people,
he brought forth fountains of faith
as pure as the waters of Meribah.

We have come to an age of drought,
a wilderness of thirst,
where the springs of faith
trickle into the desert sands
and are lost.

Let us return to stand in the cool shadow
of the enduring rock of our people,
waiting, speaking, even striking
so the waters of faith
will flow from it again.

The New Moon

NUMBERS 25-30

If God were the sun, then Israel might be
the moon,
her face reflecting His eternal light.

Yes, Israel is like the moon, the moon
who waxes and wanes,
grows old, and then renews herself,
yet never leaves the skies.

Faithfully, she reappears to walk the night,
glimmering, silver, in the darkened sky,

Faithfully, she spreads her pale and ghostly light
on every room and tree and blade of grass

Until the whole world turns to silver,
transformed from darkness to shimmering beauty.

Yes, Israel, be like the moon,
renew your faith each generation.

Even when the earth casts its shadow of
darkness,
faithfully reflect the light of God;

Pour over the whole world
the moonlight beauty of holiness.

Reuben and Gad

NUMBERS 32:14-16

And they stepped up to him and said: "We will build here sheepfolds for our flocks, and towns for our little ones; . . ."

And Moses said: "Build towns for your children, and sheepfolds for your flocks;"

By a simple inversion of word order
Moses corrected the leaders of Gad and Reuben,

Telling them they must build houses for their
children before they built barns for their cattle.

Though his forces were decimated from battling
Midian and he faced a new campaign in Canaan

Though he must lead his desert wanderers
against the established kings of the land

Neither military necessity nor the uncertainties
of desert life stopped Moses from teaching that
children come before sheep, human values before
property.

The city we build may have pillars of ivory and
gold, pavements of sapphire, and silken curtains
shot with color,

But we build in vain unless we build
gates of thanksgiving and windows of praise,
gardens of contemplation, and walls of love
to shelter the little ones.

To the Jordan River

NUMBERS 33

There were generations of Jews
who prayed to return to the land,

There were generations of us who longed
for Jerusalem,
who suffered and wept when we remembered
her,

There were generations who struggled for
Zion,
who contended with fellow-Jews and with
the rulers of many nations.

To us has come the age the others longed for,
the age they prayed for, suffered for,
and worked for;

To us, who are neither deserving enough,
nor grateful enough, nor understanding enough,
has come this age for greatness:
the age to rebuild Zion.

We have gone up to the land to cultivate it,
to build cities and harbors, villages and
schools, a life of goodness and abundance
for our people.

We built terraces for vineyards,
dragging the rough rocks with our bare hands,
and where the mountainsides were too steep
for vine or olive, we planted Jerusalem pine,
that sends its roots deep into the rocky hills.

Day by day and step by step we labored,
rejoicing when we saw the scarlet poppies
growing wild on the hillsides, the land
answering us, cheering us on.

Oh God Who watched over every generation
that struggled toward this age,
make us strong to build the terraces of peace,
stone on stone;
root us like Jerusalem pine in the traditions
of Israel;

Then let joy spring from our spirits,
as red poppies from the holy hills,
as we work to rebuild Zion.

God's Tenderness

DEUTERONOMY 1

Rashi wrote that God bore Israel,
not as an infant that must be carried,
but as a son who walks beside his father
through the wilderness.

When the pillar of smoke went before Israel,
it was like a father leading a son;

When the pillar of cloud remained behind them
to blind the Egyptian pursuers,
it was like a father who remains behind his son
when wild animals are following them;

Like a father, God put himself between Israel
and every threatening danger;
like a father He held Israel on his arm
while they fought their enemies.

I will seek You, not because of Your power
nor Your majesty,
but because You are like a father
who guards his son.

I will pray to You, not because of Your wonders
or Your miracles
but because of Your tenderness
which is like the tenderness of a mother
for her daughter.

I pray to be like that child.
Though danger and hardship are my lot
I would walk with the sure knowledge
of my parents' loving care.

The Funnel of Time

DEUTERONOMY 3-7

I prayed to my ancient Lord:
return me to Sinai,
make me a sister to Joshua,
a son to Moses, a child of Israel once again,
to listen, to understand, to perform.

Pour us back through the funnel of time
to Sinai—
my children, my parents, my grandparents—
remove from the earth the scars of the cities
we inhabit;

Remove from our memories the many times
we have turned away from You;
Return us all, as children, to begin again,
to hear this time, to understand this time;
this time to obey.

Yes, You are the One who pardons and forgives,
but forgiveness contains no gift of innocence,
and You will not return me to the beginning;

You will not roll time back for my people,
nor erase history from the consciousness
of the peoples of the earth.

Turn Your face toward us, Lord of the universe,
renew Your revelation, as You gave it at Sinai,

Soften our hearts that we may return to You,
hear us in our repentance,

Let Your Torah be the compass that turns us
toward righteousness, toward compassion, and toward
  You.

Lessons of the Wilderness

DEUTERONOMY 10:12

*And now, Israel, what is it that the Lord your God
demands of you? It is to revere the Lord your God, to
walk only in His paths, to love Him, and to serve the Lord
your God with all your heart and soul.*

You Who are Lord of all nature,
why do You concern Yourself with humanity?

What is Israel that You should command us
to revere You, to serve You and to love You?

In the days of affliction, we call to You,
and from the wastelands of despair we cry to You,

But when You test us with wealth and might,
our pride comes near to blotting out our prayer.

If we are to serve You with all our might,
we must use our power for others.

If we are to serve You with mind and heart,
we must study and pray.

If we are to serve You with all our souls,
even the evil inclinations must serve You.

Lord our God, though we are unworthy,
You have lifted us up with Your inspiration.

Though we wither as the grass,
You have exalted us with Your commandment
to love You.

The Choice

DEUTERONOMY 11:26

See this day I set before you blessing and curse;

Are we free as the birds?
Yes, and more free,
for birds fly by the charts of instinct
and make no choice in the pattern of their existence.

Are we free as the angels?
Yes, and more free,
for angels, if they exist, live beyond evil,
and face no agonizing choices.

Sometimes we seem like little children,
round-eyed before a holiday table, permitted
for once to reach for the sweetest cake.

But we are neither children nor winged creatures;
we are human beings. Freedom to choose is our definition,
and ability to choose well is our portion of divinity.

Gratefully we thank You
Who are the source of our freedom.
Earnestly we pray to You
when we pace the dark corridors of decision.

Let us make each choice with wisdom.
Let us choose blessing and peace.

Rules for the King

DEUTERONOMY 19-21

The king of Israel was not to be a valiant horseman,
exulting in the arched neck and bulging muscles
of his mount;

He was not to fill his stables with stallions
whose plunging hoofs and shrill screaming
are magnificent in battle;

He was not to have many royal princesses in his harem,
nor much silver and gold in his treasury.

He was to copy for himself the book which says,
"Justice, justice shalt thou pursue,"
and read it all the days of his life.

We who are sophisticated in politics, economics,
and military strategy may find it quaint

that an ancient king in a tiny country
would maintain that study would preserve him and his
children, when he had few horses and little wealth.

Only now is it alarmingly true that the scientist
who experiments with the atom
may start cancers in the bones of his own child.

Only in our day is it suddenly true
that the politician trusts in weapons
that may set afire the homes of his own people.

Only now is it so fatally true that all of us
who fail to pursue justice and demand it of our statesmen
may perish in an atomic holocaust.

We pray You set our faltering feet
on the path of peace.

Family Laws

DEUTERONOMY 22:6, 7

If, along the road, you chance upon a bird's nest, in any tree or on the ground, with fledglings and the mother sitting over the fledglings or on the eggs, do not take the mother together with her young.

Before these laws of kindness we stand in awe,
and humbly pray to become conscious
of the implications of our actions.

We must do more than spare the mother bird
to preserve the wildlife of the earth.

We must build more than parapets on rooftops
to prevent harm to others.

We must do more than return a pledge
to alleviate the misery of poverty.

We seek the insight of those who taught us
that we are created in Your image.

That an act of kindness is a blessing to You,
but an injustice defames Your name.

Whether we hire a person or work for one,
whether we buy or sell, teach or study,
let us never be a reproach to You.

Whether we are leaders or followers,
parents or children, lenders or borrowers,

We pray that the spirit of these teachings
will permeate all our relationships
with thought-filled kindness, with conscious consideration.

Remembrance

DEUTERONOMY 25

Remember, oh remember Amalek and Haman,
Hitler and Torquemada;

Remember Moses, who lost his temper,
and Esther, who tried to hide her Judaism;

Remember, oh remember that you
were a slave in the land of Egypt.

Do not forget, for memory, fluid, clouded
memory is the beginning of the future.

To remember both the good and the evil,
to love the good and understand the evil,

To uncover them in ourselves and in others,
that is the beginning of wisdom.

With memory clear, with the past understood,
we shall overcome tyranny and hatred.

We shall overcome prejudice and lust for power,
we shall overcome cruelty and fear.

Understanding the past, the key to ourselves,
we shall seek courage and wisdom,

We shall seek the hereditary portion
of all peoples, which is peace.

When we overcome the evil that is past and present,
we shall overtake the future of
peace and good for all God's children.

Across Every River

DEUTERONOMY 27:2-8

*Moses told the people of Israel that as soon as they crossed
the Jordan they should select stones, and "on those stones
you shall inscribe every word of this Teaching most
distinctly."*

How many rivers we have crossed since we crossed the
    Jordan:
The River of Babylon and the flooding Nile,

We passed over the Rubicon and the Rhine,
the Danube and the Volga,

We sailed oceans only to cross other rivers:
the Mississippi, the Amazon, the Ganges . . .

And when we crossed each river, we wrote the words,
we wrote them on scrolls and in books,

We translated them into seventy languages,
and more than seventy, as our rabbis instructed us,

No longer shepherds nor growers of vines and figs,
we transmuted our understanding of this Teaching,
to make it clear, distinct, in every time,
in every place, across every river.

And still we struggle, now where the words were first
written and in every other land where we live
to make this Torah distinct for ourselves and for Jews
everywhere.

King Josiah

DEUTERONOMY 29, 30
also II KINGS 22:1-23:30

In the Second book of Kings
we read this account of the reign of Josiah:

While the priests were supervising carpenters and masons
repairing the Temple, they found a book.

Huldah, the woman prophet, proclaimed
this book the word of God.

Filled with fear because of its curses against idolatry,
Josiah stood before his people and made them accept
the covenant of this new book: Devarim.

In the Temple were vessels made
for the gods and goddesses of Canaan.
Josiah ordered them destroyed.

He killed the idolatrous priests
and tore down the idols on the high places
throughout the land.

So Josiah turned to the Lord
with all his heart, all his soul, and all his might.

Yet the book reports that Josiah was slain at Megiddo
in battle with the Pharaoh-necho of Egypt.

When we read its litany of curses and blessings,
we cannot forget the struggle of the little state of Judea
against the great powers of the ancient world.

We accept the moral teachings of Deuteronomy,
but know we cannot expect immediate blessings and curses
for our deeds. Our tradition speaks truthfully:
Josiah, the righteous king, was killed in battle.

We can choose between good and evil—
our actions have consequences, which we must try to
  foresee,
for our tradition demands moral behavior always.

The Last Days of Moses

DEUTERONOMY 31

He who had confronted the Pharaoh of Egypt
could not hold the hand of the smallest child
when it stepped into the promised land.

He who had raised his staff to divide the Red Sea,
could not cross over
the thin stream of the Jordan.

He who had touched the hem of the garment
of God could not touch the least pebble
of the land of Israel.

He had given up his place as prince of Egypt,
had sacrificed the peace of his shepherd's life in Midian,
and had passed over his own sons
to appoint Joshua his successor.

He had sacrificed his life to his people
that they attain freedom,
and he could not enter the promised land.

No Oedipus, ignorant of his offense,
no Hamlet, caught in the irrevocable past,

Moses knew his faults and his sins.
Moses knew he must march forward
to obey the commands of God.

The deeds of Moses were great and heroic;
his tragedy was not in his death,
but in us who forsake the laws
he taught us.

Almighty God, will the history of Moses
be a sorrow forever?
Must every person and every people nullify
Your gift of freedom with some human flaw?

We pray you
bring this consolation to the soul of Moses:

That in every age there are men and women
who live like heroes, even though they perish
without setting foot in the promised land.

The Song of Moses

DEUTERONOMY 32:11

In the wilderness of Midian and the deserts of Sinai
Moses must have watched many eagles.

He had seen them, birds who mate for life,
building their great eyries high on steep mountainsides.

He had seen the keen-eyed eagle gliding in the sky,
had seen it swoop, swift and fatal, on its prey,

Yet he knew this king of birds,
this most powerful, swift and dangerous bird,
cares tenderly for its young;

The parent bird first pushes the eaglet from the nest,
then soars beneath it, ready to support the young
on its majestic wings.

So Moses thought of his God:
as the king of birds, swift and powerful,
a watcher in the skies,

A parent who prodded an infant people from the nest
    of Egypt,
protecting them on their first flight of freedom.

So Moses spoke in his great farewell:
"Like an eagle who rouses his nestlings,
Gliding down to his young,
So spread He His wings and took him,
Bore him along on His pinions;"

God alone did lead Moses and Israel
and there was no strange god with them.

Section Three
Barley

Sub Specie Aeternitas

Dream flight is bird flight, rising on beating wings,
mounting the wild inimical wind. But I rose, seated,
in a plane, watching the landscape hang at the window,
tilt, flow away, and settle into neat and daylight patterns.

Is the world so, in the eye of eternity, neat and noiseless?
Two thousand feet of air can obliterate racket and smell,
dust and human voices. My head rested
against the rubber cushion. Speed was only an idea.

                    Intellectual flight is plane flight,
rising on logic, with no sensation of history. The neat
patterns of humans evolving, the numbered trends
and causes and all
the changing technologies unroll beneath the reading eye.
I fly with ease above Babylon and Greece and falling Rome,
but over one small desert I cannot fly.

                    Sand stings my eyes,
heat dries my throat, the desert itself clings to my feet,
and I am struggling toward the mountain that rumbles
    and flames,
pouring smoke into the virgin sky where no plane flies.
Breathless, I wait there in the everlasting present
for the trumpet call and the voice.

Wingless

Our past goes back to Sinai, our future will be complete
   at Zion,
But now we live in this divided present,
Struggling for direction.

With psalms and prayers, the fine nets our people have
   woven,
we will recapture our dreams.

Dusted with powders of flight, gliding on wings of dreams,
we will return to the wilderness,
we will roam the desert of Sinai.

We have struggled to survive in heat and sand,
we have been hungry and afraid and angry.

Now we stand at Sinai, the earth rumbles,
flames roar from the mountain, trumpets scream.

Above the thunder, the crashing of rocks, the quaking
   of earth,
beyond the rage and fright trembling within us,

We hear the voice of God.

With fear we promise to obey the commandments,
with awe we accept the responsibility of Torah,
with humility we take our places among the people of Israel.

Wingless now, we are dropped
in the howling wilderness of our present

Knowing that when we hear and obey
we go forward toward Zion,

When we live by the word of God
we have reached the foot of the mountain,

When we love the Lord our God
we will come to exultation.

When We Stood at Sinai

When we stood at Sinai we promised:
"We will hear and we will obey."

> Now we stand at Auschwitz and we promise: "We will remember human deeds and we will seek understanding."

At Sinai we heard the revelation of God who spoke to Moses and to us.
At Auschwitz we seek the revelation of God who is silent and hidden.

> We will cherish the memory of those who died as martyrs, and the memory of those who died resisting, and especially of those who died in terror.

We mourn our dead, our twice dead, dead once in the gas chambers, dead again in the dripping chambers of our hearts.

> We will listen to the testimony of every witness, we will search among the books and the documents, among the very stones of Europe and Israel.

To find again the sparks of holiness, the undying sparks of the Jewish spirit.

> Mourning our dead, we cannot be silent. Mourning them, we are forced into the jaws of politics, into the canine teeth of empire.

Mourning them, we make ourselves responsible for history, for we believe that the kingdom of God depends on human deeds.

> We affirm our belief that we can choose life, as Moses told us. We affirm our belief that we can choose freedom, as America promises us.

We affirm our belief that our mourning and our remembering will strengthen our work for peace and justice, even in the face of Auschwitz.

We affirm our belief that we can hear, we can understand, and we can act, as we repeat the words we said at Sinai: *Shema Yisrael Adonai Eloheinu, Adonai Eḥad!*

Snow Scene

The snow was dazzling in the sun,
The shadows blue, bright blue the air;
I thought as I have often thought:
Thank God for setting beauty there.
Then all at once felt self-accused
And found no virtue in my prayer.

Must I see beauty ere I think of God?
Does my heart thank because my eyes behold?
When I thought what I thanked Him for
I felt the snow's inhuman cold.

You know my heart is blind,
And I must use my eyes to see,
But those who lived in ghetto streets
Saw little beauty, yet loved Thee.

My age wants gifts and evidence,
Unlike those folk of long ago,
We lack the knowledge of Your love
Within our hearts, a steady glow
That could replace the need for proofs.

I tell my old demands and doubts: Depart!
Now let me pray with seeing, knowing heart.

Rich Signs

Yellow warblers flit through the garden
swinging and dipping and rising;
swallows fly swift and true as arrows;

> Hawk and falcon rise on invisible air currents
> higher and higher, soaring into the heavens.

How our souls long to fly upwards,
released from the earth, like flying birds!

> Swinging and dipping, the warbler
> finds insects and seeds to eat;
> and the swallow, her beak full of berries
> flies straight to her young in the nest.

From the heights of his vision
the hawk dives on his prey with crushing speed.

> Oh how our souls long to fly upwards
> like the flying birds!

Yet see how God dangles before us
rich signs of our inner life:

> Not released from the earth, from nesting and feeding,
> we gather strength so our souls can fly,
> seek vision, soaring higher and higher.

God of Sky and Sea

God of sky and sea, of vastness and silence,
God of mother and child, of closeness and sweetness,

What are we that we are mindful of You?
What are we that we can contemplate You?

In the universe of matter, from atom
To astronomical systems, are You recognized?

And in living things, from algae to ape,
Are You comprehended, except by human minds?

This is our distinction, Mind of the Universe,
This is our difference from all other things:

That You have hidden in this shallow skull
A capacity to think of You.

That somewhere in this complex brain
Is a compulsion to search for You.

What crown of glory is this,
To know eternity is other than ourselves?

What honor is this, to see our faults
And our sins, to know ourselves wanting in Your sight?

Is this Your blessing, that we contemplate
Good and evil, God and eternity?

Is this Your gift of faith, that having looked upon ourselves
In an agony of despair, we live, we try again?

God of sky and sea, of vastness and silence,
God of parent and child, of closeness and sweetness,

Look down at us now with love and mercy,
Help us to bear what we have seen and understood.

Master of All Worlds

Master of all worlds, the world of reality
And the world of imagination,
God of all that is created
And all that is yet to come,

Master of time and history,
You who are eternal,
Outside of time, free of dimension
And beyond the world of humanity,

Look down at Your children living in pain and hunger,
Suffering from starved and stunted imaginations.

Send us leaders with vision who work in time and history
Yet are uncorrupted by the conquest of people and their
    minds.

Lord, God of history, we know there will be no new Moses;
For him we say: Dayenu.*

But surely if You harden the heart of every Pharaoh
You must send us an Aaron to speak for us or a Miriam to
    sing for us.

Look down on Your children, God of the world,
Be again our parent and lead us from our childish ways.

*"It would have been enough"—from the Passover service

Yizkor

O Lord of Abraham and of Jesus,
Of Buddha and of Confucius,
God of those enslaved and those deified
And those who walk in restless freedom,
God of every man, woman, and child, hear us now:
Is one language better than another?
Is mathematics truer than poetry?
Is righteousness more real than physics?
How shall we know You?
What symbols can invoke You?
What senses apprehend You?
O speak to us, slave and free,
Who have made of ourselves too much,
Or not enough, O speak to us,
Face to face, as it is written,
Breath to breath, mouth to mouth.
O different we are, different You have made us,
And different we shall die, divided from one another,
Yet make us know that You are God, one God,
Who in the infinite complexity of the universe
Speaks and unites everyone who listens.

Letter to a Humanist

Men and women are the messengers of God;
There are neither angels nor emanations;
Only people like you, in whom God has planted
A striving for justice and freedom and peace.

Inspiration and dedication and every inward joy
Are the gifts of God, who makes us equal with equal love
And appoints us, every one, God's messengers and workers
To bring another springtime to the world.

Listen to your own inner conversation:
You will learn that
When you work for justice,
You are bringing redemption;
When you work for freedom and peace,
You are praying for salvation;
When you accept and love another person,
The Messiah draws near.

Out of My Need

Out of my need and my helplessness I cry to You
Knowing You are One, and we who cry are many,

Knowing that without illusions I am weak
And without rationalizations I am naked,

Knowing that before You I must cover my head
And seek to hide my thought with shame.

Knowing that You are far off, still I pray to You,
For You are the source of all help and all strength.

Love me better than I have loved,
And protect me better than I protect my own.

Teach me to pray, teach me to believe;
Teach me to be one in my heart as You are One.

I am to you nothing, You are to me God;
Therefore I beg of You: hear me, help me, teach me.

Invisible, Intangible

All the invisible things fill our days,
Music and love and laughter;
All the intangible things affect us,
Words and anger and prejudice.

You are invisible and intangible,
A God of moods and relationships.
Within us, you are the spirit of unity.
Beyond us, You are the guide to greatness.

We pray to You with an invisible, intangible prayer.
You answer with a flaming sunset
And the touch of a baby's cheek.

Books

Many books have influenced me, but the two which have affected me most are Mordecai Kaplan's *Judaism as a Civilization* and Gershom Scholem's *Major Trends in Jewish Mysticism*. The older I get, the more congenial I find Kaplan's idea of process—God as process, the universe as process, Judaism undergoing a process of religious evolution. Of course nothing stays the same, the same river always contains different waters, and the waters change the banks, . . . but it has taken me years of mature living to grasp the motion of all things, some of it as slow as stone.

Scholem gave me permission to accept mysticism as something which has long been part of Judaism, and not just the private eighteenth-century addition of the Ḥasidic movement. His work helped me to understand my own feelings and experiences as well as to understand when many Jews turned back to their traditions after the Holocaust. Kaplan and Scholem, both meticulous in their scholarship, nonetheless understood that there is a force beyond scholarship and learning. Torah and Talmud are a beginning, not an end in themselves, a dancing of definition around indefinable flames.

"The Chosen People"

Why am I different from all others?
I cried in my loneliness,

And a thousand children's voices piped,
Why are we different from all other people?

But there are no two stones alike
In all the universe of pebbles.

No two leaves on any tree are just the same,
Nor animals, nor birds, nor people.

Difference is the mark of the hand of the Creator
And evolution is God's handiwork.

Each of us is meant to be ourselves
And each people to be great in its own way.

We are different in a universe of differences
Swimming in the moving waters of history.

We Jews want to be a warm current in an icy river,
We want to create a climate for living things.

Let us have courage to be thankful for our differences,
Let us pray for strength to accept our obligations.

Demons and Ghosts

We smile at the tales that were told long ago
Of demon and dybbuk, of golem and ghost,
Of nymphs in the forest and spirits in trees.

We laugh at the demons and haunts of old times,
For we are the ones who are like our machines,
Adjusted, each one, to the work we must do.

Yes, we are the fools who deny all our demons
And live like a piston propelled by explosions
And die like a clock with a broken-down mainspring.

But deep in our souls is the voice of the spirit
That weeps and imagines, that dreams and demands,
That seeks for the marvel and terror of God,

Whose wonders began on the day of creation,
Whose spirit is set in our souls like a spell,
Who calls us to reach from the shadows toward Light.

Oh Lord, turn us back to the truly mysterious,
The magic of art and the miracle, love.
Oh give us Your hand when we leap from the darkness.

The Gift of Speech

Almighty God, withdraw Your ancient curse of Babel,
Remove from us the confusion of tongues.

For we have built radar towers and trusted in them,
Bombs and missiles, and put our faith in them.

Curse us no more with dumb power,
Remove from us these speechless weapons.

Bless us with the blessing of language
So there can be speech even among those who are angry.

Bless us with the blessing of understanding
So even prejudiced people can understand.

Grant us the divine power of words, Holy One,
That we may speak with our brothers and sisters.

Open their ears that they may hear us,
Open their hearts that they may understand us.

Open their mouths that they may answer,
Open our ears and our hearts that our mouths may respond.

O return unto all Your children speech—
That we may once more speak together as a peaceful family.

Fingerprints

Though You are the God of History
and earthquakes and thunder and tidal waves,

Though I do not doubt Your majesty and power,
Your magnitude and Your abstractness,

Though You are hallowed far beyond my imaginings,
so that I can hardly exalt You or sanctify You,

> I sometimes think of You as the "God of my fathers;"
> Surely my grandfather believed You guided his feet
> when he carried the peddler's pack.

> And surely You put the twinkle
> in his eye when he spoke of his life.

> You put the righteousness in my father's soul,
> like a burning star, and laughter in his mouth,
> a bubbling spring.

> Surely it was You who set in the heart of my little son
> pity for a small stray dog, and You
> who gentled his hand to pet it.

God of my fathers and my sons, You mark us with
> Your fingerprints:
courage and righteousness, laughter, gentleness and pity.

I seek your imprint, to cherish it.

Timor Temporis

God of mercy and lovingkindness,
Hear me now and in the days to come;
Be gracious to me now and in the time of pain and
   remorse;
Comfort me when old age weakens my mind and saps
   my strength,
When the rich fruits of life wither and sour,
When loneliness is the guest at my table.
Lord God You know my naked soul.
Be with me now,
Be with me at the hour of death.

God, You Listen

God, You listen to prayer.
Hear our prayers when they
are worth listening to.

God, You are one.
Hear us when we are one people.
Hear each of us when we speak as a whole person,
a single one.

God, You create.
Hear us when we try to create
a loving relationship,
or a better ground for a growing
soul, or hope.

God, You know us.
Help us to summon our souls,
to stretch with utmost love toward You.

November

The dried leaves rattle against the stone wall,
the lake is glassy for it soon will freeze.
It is a time to change.

The squirrels look fat with their thicker fur,
the cat curls in the warmth behind the kitchen stove.
It is a time to think.

The sun sets early behind the snow-filled clouds,
the trees stand in their nakedness to receive the snow.
It is a time to remember.

It is a time to remember that winter will pass.
It is a time to think of ways to keep warm through the dreary
    months.
It is a time to change.

For though there is ice underfoot,
the climate of the heart may be warm and welcoming.

Though deep snow lies at the door,
the soul may be warm in the radiance of God.

The Ringed Hand

Power was once the special poison of kings
and luxury their peculiar corruption.

The ringed hand that held the scepter
could command a treasury of wealth.

The gloved hand that bore the falcon
could signal death for any of its subjects.

But now, buried beneath their crumbling castles
lie the kings who rode across the bloody years.

Some mad, some merely weak and silly,
all as obsolete as their rusted armor.

Yet envy them their harmlessness
whose treasuries held gold, not oil nor uranium,

whose armorers forged sword and spear
and never heard of missile or H-bomb.

Who now is corrupted with power
and poisoned with luxury?

Whose hands can rob the earth of its treasures
and make desolate its lands?

Whose finger can push the button
marked simply "death for all"?

We, the uncrowned, we the people,
astride the apocalyptic beast
galloping across this century,

While strapped to our wrist, its talons piercing the flesh,
rides the hideous hooded bird, that released,
would rise, screeching, to blacken the sky forever.

A Bloodroot Blossoming

Here where I knelt in stillness I kneel again
Remembering woodland where I walked in spring,

I trod the frozen slush and damp leaf mold
And found a bloodroot blossoming in a clod of snow;

Here where I thought I heard him once, I wait again
For the true words of the unknown messenger.

Master of messengers, I beg, send me a gift of moments:
Discovery, like a flower in snow; stillness, like a prayer at
    night.

Yet here where I wait there is no stillness; my heart beats
    loud,
I hear the crackling of the cold in the walls of my house,

And I doubt there is any final truth to be discovered
In our world of leaf mold and blossom, growth and decay.

Like all the others, I learned of stillness through suffering
And of truth when I felt the twisted knife of falsehood.

Oh God, I will no longer ask You for moments of peace
But I will pray for the right choice at moments of decision.

I will not ask for the messenger to reveal Your truth
But I will pray to discover courage at moments of trial.

Jewish Beginnings

When Joshua led the tribes of Israel
into the promised land,
it was a great beginning.

The Jordan stopped flowing.
The tribes marched over, trumpets blaring,
drums pounding, priests bearing the ark,
everyone singing, "Hallelujah, hallelujah."
It was a magnificent moment, the dream realized,
the beginning of life in the promised land.

Yet we do not celebrate that beginning,
but rather the moment when our ancestors,
frightened slaves, fled Egypt at midnight
for the desert wilderness.

We mourn the destruction of the Temple,
the city of Jerusalem in flames,
the Romans' battering rams destroying walls and houses.

We thought it was an ending; some of us still do.
Did anyone notice a few ragged people
bearing a coffin out of the city?
Few knew until long afterwards
that the man inside the coffin was alive, *
a teacher who would start a school in a little town.
That was the beginning we should remember:
the beginning of Talmud, of rabbinic Judaism.

Beginnings hide in endings;
out of chaos comes new creation.

When the Jews were exiled from Spain,
long lines of refugees fled along the road,
some on foot, some in carts,

*Yoḥanan ben Zakkai

making for harbors and ships to take them away,
carrying their bundles and their babies
and weeping, weeping.

How many knew that the same cruel queen
who exiled them had sent an obscure explorer
with three small ships to find a western route to India?

How many knew there was a Jew aboard
that first ship to touch America,
the land of our shelter, of our growth?

When an unimportant French army captain,
loyal to his country, an assimilated Jew,
was tried for treason, an anti-Semitic event
not nearly so bloody as the Czar's pogroms . . .
Who knew a Viennese journalist would be set afire
with a dream of Zion restored, a Jewish state?
The Dreyfus case and Theodor Herzl—
a small shame that became a great beginning.

Hiding in America today, where we fear ending,
assimilation, lost loyalties and ignorance,
new Jewish life is stirring, is awakening, is beginning.
We search and fumble and seek answers,
new prayers, new ways to be Jews.

In another century, Jews will look back
and see that we too made a new,
a great beginning.

Who Are These Jews?

There were women who sat in the market
selling beets and cabbages so their men could study:
they were Jews.

There were men of Yemen, great swordsmen,
guards of the king: they were Jews.

There are dark women from India, wearing saris,
black farmers from Ethiopia,
children with slanted eyes: all Jews.

There are dressmakers and sculptors,
thieves and philanthropists, scholars and nurses
beggars and generals.

There are women who follow every rule of Kashrut
and men who know none of the rules,
yet all of us are Jews.

Though we are not alike in mind or body,
somewhere in the depths of our souls
we know we are the children of one people.

We share a history, a hope, and some prayers;
We speak many languages;
We have heard one Voice:

All of us stood together at Sinai
When our past and our future
Exploded in thunder and flame before us.

The Tyranny of Time

Are we to be slaves of time for all our days?
Shall the past ordain our future and history our fate?

God, You have the power to open our eyes,
To let us see our past with Your compassion,

Have power to break the binding chains of guilt,
To let us choose a different, better life.

And even the consequence of sin and error,
With God to help us, is not inevitable.

You have power to change the stream of history:
In our day exile has become return.

This is our miracle and sign and wonder:
That Jews left death in other lands for life in Israel.

Your power is great, and Your message is hope.
Help us to end the tyranny of time
By looking at our guilty past in Your true light.

Help us to lay fate aside and choose redemption,
Help us to put destiny away and choose salvation,
Help us to create our future according to Your ways.

Network

When we walk with nature as a friend
we learn how the great chains of life intersect,

> How we live in a three-dimensional network
> including every living thing from algae to elephants,
> and these dependent on the soil, the tides, the moon,

When we walk slowly with nature, learning and under-
standing, we can grow more food, live longer, humanize
our cities, enjoy the blossoming countryside.

> When we make mistakes, we see them:
> fish dying in oil spills,
> broken eggshells that threaten a silent spring.

We have learned the lesson of our time:
life is interdependent; life is fragile.

> When we walk with other Jews as friends
> seeing our people as a living people,
> we learn how the long chains of our history intersect.

We sense that we live in a three-dimensional network
connecting Jews in Israel, in America, in Russia, every-
where in the world.

> Now we hear the message of this century
> to the Jew; life is fragile; life is interdependent.

Although we make mistakes,
an invisible network of history, commitment and witness,
part of each of us, yet greater than all of us,
keeps us in life and sustains us here and everywhere.

Sheheḥiyanu

We thank You, Eternal God
for telling us,
"My love around you,
My blessings on you
have surely brought you
to this day."

A Mother's Prayer at the Naming of Her Daughter

To carry a child in this threatening world takes faith,
to give birth to a child in this frightening world takes
love,
To raise a child to be a Jew takes courage.

Today I celebrate the gift of life
which can be accepted only with faith, love and courage,

Today I remember Sarah, who watched Abraham
when he took her only son Isaac to be sacrificed,
and I remember the covenant of Abraham, the pain of
    Sarah.

Today I remember the wife of Noah, the mother of three
children, who though she has no name in our Torah,
witnessed the suffering of her sisters, the destruction
of all her human brothers, and I remember
the covenant of Noah.

I remember that the Talmud says: one who takes a
    single life destroys the whole world.
And I say: therefore, she who gives birth creates a whole
world,
and she feels a little of the divine joy of Elohim,
creating the earth and every living thing.

Today I name my daughter a Hebrew name and an
    English name,
because I have found the courage to raise her as a Jew.
In this same ceremony I pledge her and myself to the
    Covenant
of Noah, to work for a world which will nurture life
and not destroy it.

All Jews must enter the covenant of Noah,

as my daughter will do when she learns she is mature enough
to conceive and give birth;
Both women and men must promise to protect and nurture
all living things.

All Jewish children should enter the covenant of Abraham,
as a boy does when he is circumcised.
Girls and boys alike need to learn Torah and commit themselves
to the Jewish people.

We will gather our people together to work for a world
which we will not destroy with fire or nuclear winter
or atomic missiles;
Beginning today we must work together for a world that is safe
for my baby and for all babies everywhere.

When my daughter grows up and decides to give birth, she will
find, as I do, that whatever causes pain to her child hurts her.

If all men and women learn to feel the suffering of others,
life can be preserved on this planet.

Faith and love and courage can prevail over threats and fear
and violence.

Nations will study peace and people will learn to love one another.
Despite our pain, we will work for a world of peace,
In trembling, we will raise our children as Jews,
In fear, we will insist on celebrating life,
on embracing the covenant of Noah and the covenant
of Abraham,
we and our children, and, God helping us, our children's children.

A Mother's Prayer at Her Son's Circumcision

To carry a child in this threatening world takes faith,
To give birth to a child in this frightening world takes
love,
To raise a child to be a Jew takes courage.

Today I celebrate the gift of life
which can be accepted only with faith, love and courage.

Today I remember Sarah, who watched Abraham
when he took her only son Isaac to be sacrificed,
and I remember the covenant of Abraham.

Today I remember the wife of Noah, the mother of three
sons,
who, though she has no name in our Torah, witnessed
the suffering of her sisters, the destruction of her
brothers, and I remember the covenant of Noah.

I remember that the Talmud says: one who takes a
single life
destroys the whole world.
And I say: therefore, she who gives birth creates a whole
world,
and she feels a little of the divine joy of Elohim,
creating the earth and every living thing.

Today I give my son to enter the covenant of Abraham
because I have found the courage to raise him as a Jew.
In this same ceremony I pledge myself to the Covenant
of Noah, to work for a world which will nurture life and not
destroy it.
All Jewish children should enter the covenant of Abraham,
as a boy does symbolically when he is circumcised;

Girls and boys alike need to learn Torah and commit
    themselves
to the Jewish people.

All Jews must enter the covenant of Noah,
as a young woman does when she learns she is mature
    enough to
conceive and give birth;
Both women and men must promise to protect and nurture
all living things.

We will gather our people together to work for a world
    which
we will not destroy with fire or nuclear winter
or atomic missiles;
Today we must work together for a world that is safe for my
baby and all babies everywhere.

A mother learns at her baby's circumcision that she suffers
the pain of her child, so recently parted from her.
If all men and women learn to feel the suffering of others,
life can be preserved on this planet.

Faith and love and courage can prevail over threats and
    fear
and violence.

Nations will study peace and people will learn to love one
another.

Despite our pain, we will work for a world of peace,
In trembling, we will raise our children as Jews,
In fear, we will insist on celebrating life,
on embracing the covenant of Noah and the covenant
of Abraham,
we and our children and, God helping us, our children's
children.

Section Four
Pomegranates: For the Holy Days

Sabbath Prayer

Lord, help us now to make this a new Shabbat.
After noise, we seek quiet;
After crowds of indifferent strangers,
We seek to touch those we love;
After concentration on work and responsibility,
We seek freedom to meditate, to listen to our inward selves.
We open our eyes to the hidden beauties
and the infinite possibilities in the world You are creating;
We break open the gates of the reservoirs
of goodness and kindness in ourselves and in others;
We reach toward one holy perfect moment of Shabbat.

For Kabbalat Shabbat

Praise be You, Eternal One our God, Ruler of the universe,
Who with Your word brings on the evening twilight . . .
rolling away the light before the darkness.

The trees are silent, and the earth is still,
the sun makes no sound; no voice has the hill.

The earth rolls in silence, the stars pierce the sky,
the moon will not whisper, the clouds cannot sigh.

And though God has bid them, we have not heard,
this night has fallen without sound of God's Word.

Yet Your law sends the stars across the night,
the earth turns surely from darkness to light.

How then shall we praise God who silently gives?
Each silently praises who righteously lives,

Our stillness is praise when our ears have heard
the command of love: God's unspoken word.

A Response to "Ayshet Ḥayil" for Sabbath Evening

THE WIFE TO HER HUSBAND

A good family is a special, a wonderful thing:
people who trust each other,
who care for each other.

A good family means people who listen
Who open their hearts and their minds to each other.

Each member of the family is an important person
Each with responsibilities to the others.

Some work in the home and some work outside it,
but all work together,
all grow and learn,
each in a different way.

A good family is a divine blessing
to be treasured and enjoyed.
With thanks in our hearts, we pray to find the ways
always to be a good family.

Illuminations

I can begin with a prayer of gratitude for all that is
   holy in my life.
God needs no words, no English or Hebrew, no semantics
   and no services,
But I need them.

Through prayer, I can sense my inner strength, my inner
   purpose,
my inner joy, my capacity to love.
As I reach upward in prayer, I sense these qualities
in my Creator.

To love God is to love each other, to work to
   make our lives better.
To love God is to love the world He created and to
   work to perfect it.

To love God is to love dreams of peace and joy that
   illumine all of us,
and to bring that vision to life.

Memory

Loaded with everything I have done,
Burdened with suffering I have caused
and the suffering I have endured,
I take breath and plunge into the dark cold sea.

Deeply, swiftly the burden pulls me down
past the ghostly fish and the waving reeds
to a murky depth where I glimpse a gleaming jewel
half hidden in the mud.

I grasp it, let go my burden, and begin to rise;
Rapidly I rise, feeling You draw me upward
until I breach the surface and fill my bursting lungs.

Light fills the sky and shines on the moving waters.
The world You made lies before me like a great Torah,
mystery and love rolled up within it.

Your light sets the jewel in my hand afire,
sparkling with my purest dreams.

Filled with the breath of life, dazzled with light,
overflowing with love—
Your love reaching toward me, my love reaching toward
  You,
the love of all for one another—

Lord God, at this moment I have returned to You,
and You have returned me to life.

Kol Nidre

Turning and returning
    this melody flows
Calling and recalling
    bringing us home

    Turning and returning us
        to other years
    Calling us to remember
        and dream once more.

        In the dreaming and remembering
            In the winding flow of time
        We hear the weeping of Marranos
            who were torn from our people
        And yet returned to us.
            Across the cruel centuries
            They call these words: "We were not lost
                nor shall you be lost,
            "We were not destroyed,
                nor shall you be destroyed,
            "You shall be forgiven your false vows
                as we were forgiven,
            "You shall be returned again
                to your people and your homes."

    Flowing around the turning earth,
        This prayer unites us wherever we live:
    Some in exile and some redeemed,
        Some in safety and some in danger;
    We are one people, praying together.

    Kol Nidre returns us to our past
        to the home of our ancestors.

Kol Nidre turns us toward the future,
toward the unknown homes of our children.

Call to us and change us,
O Lord, on this night,
Turn us, as we sing this prayer,
and we shall return to You.

Selihot

In darkening shade
lies city street,
in deepening shadow
wood and meadow,
and barren and shallow
our thoughts tonight.

> Through blackened window
> through tight closed door
> no wind can wander,
> no light can enter,
> empty our hearts
> and fallow and blight.

Now do we ask of You
deep in Your universe,
far in Your wanderings,
Maker so merciful,
Open Your cloudbanks
to moon full and bright.

> Let moonlight
> illumine us,
> night winds
> come brushing us,
> breath of Your presence
> be felt in our souls.

Footnote to a Rosh Hashanah Prayer

Like the rays of the late afternoon sun
Slanting through the trees, shining on each separate leaf,
You shine on us, our God,
And like the leaves we reflect Your light.

I thank You with all my heart
For the presence of Your spirit, which is life.
I pray You not to withdraw from me,
I pray You not to depart from me, though I am unworthy,
I pray You let me pray to You.

How can I love You, who are so far away?
How can I know You, whose face I have not seen?
How can I approach You, when my time is so short?

I can love some of Your creatures, and so love something
   of You.
I can know some of Your world, and so know something
   of You.
I can approach You with repentance and prayer and
   righteous deeds,
But I can do none of these, my God, without Your help.

Help me to love You and know You and pray to You
That this my existence may become a life,
A life that like a leaf in the afternoon sun
Reflects Your great and golden light.

Sh'ma Kolenu

You created us, and You can destroy us with floods,
with advancing glaciers, or with some small cosmic change
that might irradiate the atmosphere or boil the oceans.

You could destroy us all at once, though we will each,
sooner or later, be destroyed—by ourselves,
by each other, or by You.

My world will end, and soon.
It is one in the infinity of different worlds You made,
and the only one I helped to make.
The memory of my world will soon be gone.

Yet we play with atoms and disease bombs,
indulge ourselves in race riots,
eradicate plants, insects and animals, including ourselves.

We study war, we research destruction, we dream of death.

Would You consider us heirs of Your promise to Noah?
Is the arching rainbow archaic,
now that we can project the path of a satellite travelling
    through
the galaxy?

And if You plan to keep Your promise to Noah,
that simple archaic man,
How do You plan to make US keep it?

Why does it seem better to me, Lord God of the universe,
that we die one at a time instead of all at once?

Why do I, whose world will be destroyed,
now suddenly plead with You for all the other imperfect
    human worlds
that will follow mine?

Why do I pray for life to continue? Why do I beg:
Withhold the hands that destroy, Yours or ours?

It is because of the astonishing color of a sumac bush blazing
outside my window,
It is because of the laughter of my little boy,
running in the sunlight, trying to capture the golden leaves.

It is because of Abraham who taught us to plead with You:
I, too, have known people who are good.

The Shofar Calls

The shofar calls: Tekiah
    Arise! Awake! Come from your beds, your homes
    to the blast that calls you,
    the siren that warns you:
    seek shelter for your spirit,
    enter now the opening gates.

The ram's horn cries: Shevarim
    Worship in truth, pray together
    in confidence and in trust,
    determined that promises shall be kept,
    oaths fulfilled, words spoken thoughtfully
    in honor and in truth.

The shrill notes tremble: Teruah
    Listen to the cries of the ancient martyrs,
    Sense the unbearable silence of the dead,
    Contemplate in reverence and awe
    all those who died "L'kiddush ha-Shem."

The shofar blasts: Tekiah gadolah
    Remember! Recall the ages of our people,
    Dwell on your own life in the year that has passed,
    Call up from the darkness the mistakes, the errors,
    the evil deeds that you must deal with now.

Three times three the great horn blows: Tekiah, shevarim,
    teruah
    Return! Return to God Who made you,
    Arise to prayer, awake to memory, achieve repentance.
    Return to God Who loves you,
    Now while the days of awe are passing,
    before the closing of the gates.

In the Fall

In the fall, in the fall
When the leaves are red as blood,
When the butterflies are dust,
We repent us of our sins.
And our sins are very great,
Greater than the sins of our ancestors.

We had six million brothers and sisters
Who perished in the night.
In that long and shrieking night
We had six million brothers and sisters
Who summoned no angels, witnessed no miracles,
Who suffered and died.

We reached out our hands to our brothers and sisters,
But our hands were feeble and saved only a few.
We Jews lost the war.
We mourn our dead, our twice dead:
Dead once in the gas chambers,
Dead again in the dripping chambers of our hearts.

We repent the weakness of our hands,
We resolve to strengthen them.
Oh, our brothers and our sisters,
Mourning you, we have no rest.
Mourning you, we cannot be dumb.
Mourning you, we are forced
Into the jaws of self-analysis,
Into the claws of politics,
Into the canine teeth of empire.

After their world ended with a bang,
We were glad to hear the whimper of a lost child,
A child left to us to save.

And after the gas chambers
(No angels carried the children from the fiery furnace)
Afterwards there was this small, homemade amateur miracle:

This stubborn sturdy wonder
Growing on a harsh, dry foreign coast,
This slight, unlikely State of Israel,
Ready to take the whimpering child.

Two million brothers and sisters
Speaking an old harsh tongue
Living in this half-born state
Practicing miracles, learning to cope with history.

Wasn't it easier, Barak, to win battles
In the day when the stars in their courses
Fought against your enemy, against Sisera,
When the mountains could skip like rams to help you?

But now the sun rises daily, the stars rotate systematically,
And earthquakes, often predictable,
Duly register on seismographs
While the ḥaluẓim are sweating it out
On the dry dunams
Creating their personal miracle.

In those days, Deborah and Barak,
We swam in an ocean of the unknown,
And God was all around us.
Now, scientists all, Jew and Gentile, we stand
On the solid ground of proven fact,

Ignoring the ocean that whispers at our feet.
True, we have left God a place beyond telescope and
    microscope
Where God may guide the random atom
Or cause mutations in the genes of plants.

Meanwhile we make ourselves responsible for history,
For our six million dead brothers and sisters
And for every living, sweating brother and sister
Anywhere on this whole unpredictable planet.

Because we have no way to measure it
We ignore the ocean of the unknown
That whispers at our feet,
The ocean that holds in suspension
The dread secrets of the human heart,
That is fed by the gushing springs of destruction,
Whose waters lap the cave where maid is sacrificed to
    Minotaur.

If this sea again erupts,
Flooding gray salt water over solid land,
Leaving no island, fellow scientists,
Who will divide it for us?

In fall, when leaves are red as blood,
When butterflies are dust,
We remember our sins and repent us of our arrogance
Which is greater than the arrogance of our ancestors.

Come, let us consider our experiments,
Evaluate our hypotheses, examine our assumptions;
In short, recognize our sins and vanities,
Forego weeping and sackcloth and ashes—for those
Are the privileges of other days—
And start anew our struggle to master history,

For the Kingdom of God is to be our doing.
And we know that after the mushroom-cloud bang
There would be no single whimper.

In the recesses of our souls
Knowing full well the vast measure of the unknown,

The treachery of the human heart, even ours,
And the finality of death,
In the fall, in the time of blood and dust,
Of penitence and remembrance,
We urgently pray for the gifts of God,
Which are courage and love,
Order in the world,
Grace in ourselves,
And wisdom to worship our God.

1950

Return

HOSEA 14:2, 3, 6, 7; 11:1, 3

"Return, O Israel to the Lord your God
For you have fallen because of your sin."

> Return, as the shrill sound of the shofar
> That rises from the spiral of the ram's horn
> toward heaven.

"Take words with you and return to the Lord."

> Return, as an eagle flies, in a mounting spiral
> to its mountain nest, swift and sure.

"I will be to Israel like dew;
He shall blossom like the lily."

> Return, as the leaves in spring, renewed and beautiful.

"I fell in love with Israel
When he was still a child;
And I have called (him) My son
Ever since Egypt . . .
I have pampered Ephraim
taking them in My arms."

> Stretch out your arms to God and return,
> like a child to her mother, to love and peace.

The Watchtower

We are watchmen now
climbing the winding stairs
in the tower of David.
 At every turn we peer
 through a narrow slit
 in the thick stone wall.
  At every turn we see
  some little part of the city
  where we live out our lives.
   Climbing is hard for us,
   Our knees tremble,
   We are dizzy from the height.
  But as we climb
  We can see more—
  a broken wall on the west—
  we must repair it.
 Houses crowded against a wall
 on the South—
 we must tear down that wall
 to make room for growth.
Higher now,
we watch the first glimpse
of the ominous darkness
beyond the walls.
 Ascending the winding stairs
 we have entered
 the spiral of repentance and return.
  From a window high in this tower
  watchmen have sometimes seen
  an army gathered to besiege the city,
  although we are searching
  for an approaching messenger.

If we can reach the top, we shall see it all:
Above, the bright stars that Abraham saw.
Below, the twinkling lights of our city,
While approaching us from beyond the walls and
    the hills
shall come the messenger of the Messiah.

Ya'aleh

Night and day follow one another
like the coils of a tightly wound spring,
so nearly identical one forgets
the power for change that lies within them.

The years follow one another
so close and so alike
that forty years in the wilderness
seemed to Moses like a flight on eagles' wings.

The day, Yom Kippur, is like a person's life:
it begins in darkness and ends in darkness:
it has a time to prepare, a time to labor,
and a time to reflect before the closing of the gates.

The years follow one another
alike as the coils of a tightly wound spring,
But on Yom Kippur we think of our power
to release that spring: to soar upward!

Avinu Malkenu: Our Father, Our King

*Our Father, our King, inscribe us in the book of life, Our
Father, our King, inscribe us in the book of freedom and
salvation.*

Our Father, our King, the book of death lies open before us,
and it begins with six million names,

Our Creator, our Ruler, the book of human life lies open
before us,
but who shall judge and who shall be judged?

*Our Father, our King, we have sinned before Thee,
Our Father, our King, we have no king but Thee.*

Our Mother, our Queen, can we believe that you are a
ruler who
punishes for sin? Could any sins have deserved Auschwitz?

Our Creator, our Ruler, since you did not intercede at
Hiroshima or at Auschwitz, how are we to proclaim your
majesty throughout human history?

Our Mother, our Father, in this altered world we stand,
dimly sensing Your help and longing for it.

Our Father, our Mother, can we who were betrayed by the
whole world,
and who face betrayal again, survive through loyalty?

Our Parent, our Creator, we who have been slaughtered
survive
by standing for the sanctity of life.

Our Father, our King, we Jews are surviving history,
we live by insisting on our identity as Jews.

We stand as witnesses to the endurance of the Jews and of
every force inside us that resists another Auschwitz,
another Hiroshima.

Our Father, our King, forgive our iniquities,
Our Father, our King,
efface in Thine abundant mercy all record of our guilt.

Our Father, our King, we have been taught that Your
fatherhood means forgiveness and lovingkindness toward
Your human children.

Our Mother, our Queen, we are grown children: guilt and
forgiveness lie within us, in our hearts and in our deeds.
Our Father, our Mother, our Creator, though we no longer
   feel like
children before You, we have learned to understand that all
human beings are Your children.

Our Father, our Mother, help us not to turn our faces away
from people in need, in every part of the world.

Our Father, our Mother, we have learned that we must
forgive each other, as a parent forgives little children,
with abundant mercy.

Our Father, our Mother, You need never send another
   flood
to blot out our iniquities, but if we cannot achieve
   reconciliation,
we shall blot out all your children.

Our Father, our Mother, You need never create another
   paradise,
for if we learn to live together as a peaceful family,
earth shall become our Eden.

Our Father, our King, have mercy upon us and upon our
children. Our Father, our King, be Thou gracious unto us
and answer us. Deal with us in lovingkindness and save us.

154

We are Jews; we shall remember, and we shall survive.

We are Jews: we shall not despair of the world
nor abandon it to the forces of Auschwitz.

We are Jews. We shall remain loyal to the religion of our
    people.

Our Father, our Mother, our Creator, our Ruler, we are
    Jews.
We shall witness to the nations
that as we have endured and shall endure
so shall humankind and the world endure.

Al Ḥet

The capacity to sin is also the capacity to do good. We recite our sins together not in order to feel guilty but to learn to cope with the guilt we already feel, and to be lifted by it to a new resolve.

For the sins which we have sinned against You by misuse of ourselves:

> By neglecting and overindulging our bodies, for "the body is not less the handiwork of God than the soul,"

> > And by neglecting the mitzvot which nourish our souls,

> By failing to study Torah,

> > And also by failing to think and to use the capacities of our minds,

All these sins, O God of forgiveness, grant us the strength to confront honestly, the wisdom to analyze correctly, and the will to abandon completely, as we return to You.

For the sins which we have sinned against You and against those we love by the misuse of our capacity to love:

> By using others as objects or tools,

> > And by placing our own status and pride before the needs of others.

> By failing to use, with understanding and love, our power as employers and leaders, parents and teachers,

> > And by failing to accept with respect and love the authority of parents and teachers, employers and leaders,

By failing to perform acts of kindness, and visits to the sick and to mourners.

And by not being sensitive to others who turn to us in their need

By forming intimate relationships without love as their basis.

And also by failing to deepen love continually throughout marriage.

All these sins, O God of forgiveness, grant us the strength to confront honestly, the wisdom to analyze correctly, and the will to abandon completely, as we return to You and to those we love.

For the sins which we have sinned against You and against our community by misuse of words:

By speaking dishonestly

And by breaking promises.

By gossiping and slandering

By criticising others quickly and destructively,

. . . By keeping silent when we should have spoken.

And also by failing to praise and to thank others

All these sins, O God of forgiveness, grant us the strength to confront honestly, the wisdom to analyze correctly, and the will to abandon completely, as we return to You, to those we love, and to our community.

For the sins which we have sinned against You, against our people and against the universe You have created, by misuse of our powers:

By failing to help our own people, everywhere in the world,

And by forgetting Hiroshima and Auschwitz,

By not accepting the responsibilities of citizenship in our nation and in the international community,

And by not recognizing the fragility of our planet and the unity to all life.

By not working enough against war, poverty, violence, racism, and the dehumanization of our society.

And also by not resisting the pollution and destruction of the natural world.

All these sins, O God of forgiveness, grant us the strength to confront honestly, the wisdom to analyze correctly, and the will to abandon completely, so that we may use all our powers for good. Help us to return in joy to You, so that we may feel united in spirit with those we love, with our community and our people, with all mankind, with Your universe, and with You.

Rhythms

A cluster of lacquer-red berries falls,
A ring-necked pheasant strutting past,
Stretching his neck with strident calls,
Scatters the berries along the ground.
The wind blows hard and the snow falls fast,
The berries lie under the humus, snow-bound.

The sun shines hot and the spring rains fall,
A spear of leaf appears, then three;
Jack-in-the-pulpit prays without shawl,
And hides its pale and trembling face
Where careless wanderers cannot see
Its curving stem, its lily grace.

Preaching no message, the jack will fall
And ghostly berries appear on its stem,
Its leaves will thicken, grow large and tall,
The berries enlarge, turn lacquer-red
And fall. A pheasant will scatter them
While yellow leaves make their winter bed.

Turning and floating the oak leaves fall;
These rhythms we partially comprehend
Who find our lives patterned in all
Our days like the cycle of tree,
Of bird, and of jack, yet need to bend
And order and hold this flowing complexity.

Simḥat Torah

We have finished the Torah now,
reading of the last days of our teacher, Moses,
and we have begun at the beginning once more.

We have moved from the story of Israel
to the creation of light,
resolved to make a new and better beginning
in our study of Torah.

Before creating Adam and Eve,
God created time, evening and morning.

God created the stars and the planets whirling in their
      courses,
and the patterns of motion for earth and sun and moon.

God created plants and birds, animals and the creatures
      of the sea,
each with its beginning, its flowering, and its ending,
its rhythm of death and of birth.

Though we move in cycles, like every work of Your hand,
we are not bound to a wheel revolving on a fixed axis;
we believe we can move forward.

Inspire us, Our Creator, to continue the cycle of Torah,
strengthen us to renew the life of Israel,
help us bring Your light to our world,
speed us toward the bright morning of peace.

Sukkot

On our tables are the harvests of the earth,
pears and grapes, corn and peppers;
we thank You first for the food which sustains
us in all seasons of the year.

In winter we stand at our windows looking out
upon dreary trees;
long ago the harvest was taken, only dry stalks remain,
and frozen ground beneath the snow.

We thank You for shelter, for the body that shelters the
    spirit,
for the house and the city and the nation which shelter us.

For the talents of those who design and build,
for the ability of those who make shelters of justice
and structures of peace.

In the spring, after rain, our eyes are filled with loveliness;
greening lawn, opening bud, darting bird.

To thank You for fruitful earth and talented people
is not enough;
there is life and growth, perception,
consciousness, logic and truth,
and because of these there is Your gift of freedom.

We thank You that we are not like bud or bird,
but being human, are free to choose
even between good and evil, life and death.

In July, in the warm sweet days of summer,
we thank You for beauty.

The oaks cast their deep shadows on the lawn,
and we thank You for love:

That we dwell in the shadow of Your love,
that we are able to love,
even as You love us.

Now at Sukkot, the apples hang ripe and heavy
on the trees,
the trembling leaves shine red and gold in the sunlight.

You are the source of the radiance of the sun,
the bridegroom,
and of the fruitfulness of the earth, his bride.

For shelter and freedom, for love and beauty,
for all the harvest of earth and sun,
of talent and spirit,
For all Your blessings, we give thanks to You.

For the Blessings

For the blessings which You lavish upon us
in forest and sea, in mountain and meadow, in rain and sun,
we thank You.

For the blessings You implant within us,
joy and peace, meditation and laughter,
we are grateful to You.

For the blessings of friendship and love,
of family and community,

For the blessings we ask of You
and those we cannot ask,

For the blessings You bestow upon us openly
and those You give us in secret,

For all these blessings, O Lord of the Universe,
we thank You and are grateful to You.

For the blessings we recognize
and those we fail to recognize,

For the blessings of our tradition
and of our holy days,

For the blessings of return and forgiveness,
of memory, of vision, and of hope—

For all these blessings which surround us on every side
Dear God, hear our thanks and accept our gratitude.

Dedication

You who hold in Your hand life and earth and heaven,
You have kept Your promise of seedtime and harvest,
stormcloud and rainbow.

You have kept Your promise to us of freedom,
and daily we wrestle with the choices You have set before
us.

As for our promise to You, some make it from the
beginning
As the sunflower to the sun, or the tides to the moon.

But others must search and struggle before they achieve
dedication
As men and women seek and freely choose the ones they
love.

As the sunflower turns to the sun,
As the tides are turned by the moon,

As a woman turns to the man she loves,
So do Your people turn and return to You,

So do Your people dedicate themselves to You
Freely, and because You have willed it.

Ḥanukah

I MACCABEES 2:17-23

The light of freedom burns bright and hot
at the crossroads of decision.

In the market place at Modin
Mattathias stood in the heat and the light
for only an instant.

He heard the offer of the tyrant:
silver and gold, honor and the king's friendship,
but he, in his freedom, chose another way.

Without hesitation, he chose the law of God
for himself and his family,
though it meant warfare and death.

When we sing the holiday blessings
let us ponder the solemn choices of those men
who fathered our freedom,

When we light the Ḥanukah candles
let us remember the grave choices
freedom illuminates for us.

Ceremony of Spring

From the whispering past comes word of the ancient rites
of spring,
Tales of the goddess who sought her beloved in the
underworld:

Carnival was held to gladden the hearts of the ancient
deities of earth,
To beg from the mother-goddess fruitfulness for field and
flock and woman alike.

It is written that the daughters of Jerusalem searched the
dark city for the lover of the fairest woman,
That the maidens of Israel wept on the mountains for the
daughter of Jephtha.

We know the earth needs neither ritual nor goddess to bring
the seasons;
In due course the rotating globe will turn its cold face to
the sun.

Yet the past whispers to us when we celebrate Esther,
who walked in danger to give her people life,
When bright new dress and spicy cakes gladden the children
as they once were made to gladden the goddess.

When we crouch in the black earth planting seeds, hoping
for crops,
We make the gestures of the most ancient ceremony of
spring.

God, whose life is eternal and whose light never sets,
God, who sustains in mercy the changing seasons and
our changing souls,

I will go down to the depths of my soul to search for You,
To offer You seasonal ceremony, springtime prayer:

I will rejoice in You more than I rejoice in flower and fruit
and field.
My heart will quicken with You more than my step quickens
on the fresh grass.

I will trust in You more than I trust in the coming of summer.
I will know the warmth of Your love more than I know the
heat of the sun.

For I know that the seasons are Yours and the earth is
Yours,
You are our blessing and our hope, and we are Your
possession.

The Month of Our Freedom

The month of our freedom
shall be the beginning of all months for us,
and we who live in freedom
shall remember and rejoice in it.

In many years, in spring, the waiting earth
was stained with blood of freedom-lovers,
of Jew and Greek, of Chinese and Briton,
of the proud and the dedicated and the defeated.

At this season the sudden terror of battle
should rise to our unaccustomed throats,
forcing us to speak with pain and pride of Warsaw,
to tell with anguish and rejoicing
of the defenders of Jerusalem.

We who are weak and untested
must be born again, as our ancestors
were born in the desert of Sinai,
to responsibility and to vision.

We must bend our backs to plant the trees
in the landscape of freedom,
we must take in our hands the tools
to build the City of Peace.

Only then shall we have right and title
to rejoice in the radiant vision
of this season of remembrance, the vision
of a free people, loving and serving God.

Uncompleted Journey

Israel had gone to Egypt in time of famine
And found there food to sustain life,

Unthinking, he had accepted the power of Egypt,
Like an unhappy child, had given obedience for food,

Unknowing as a child, he had grown and learned,
Heard tales of strange gods, suffered and wondered.

Then, like a youth seeking independence from parents,
He struggled and fought for freedom.

Like an infant who must be born or strangle
Israel burst forth from the womb of Egypt,

With fear he fled through the walls of water
Leaving forever the fertile valley of the Nile.

Self-orphaned, alone and hungry, Israel fled
Into the empty desert of freedom, the rocky valleys of
    decision,

For many years he sought the God of freedom and
    righteousness,
Sought the way to the promised land where he would
    build his new home.

This is the journey of the soul: to forsake the mother's
    womb, the father's house,
To search in the wilderness for God, to build a life of
    love and independence.

This is the uncompleted journey of our people: to
    forsake slavery, to fight tyranny,

To seek the difficult ways of God, which alone teach us
    to build a world of freedom and peace.

Celebration: For the 9th of Ab

Down the centuries the prophets warned us:
The smell of burning meat cannot delight your God
nor does the odor of incense ascend to heaven.

> Rejoice, people of holiness,
> Celebrate your prophets.

Yet we clung to the ritual of the Temple,
and we brought our animals to sacrifice
like the pagans around us.

If God sent the Syrians to punish us, and the Babylonians
for our sins, surely God sent the Romans to free us
from the corrupt symbol we had made.

> Be glad, people of justice,
> Rejoice in righteousness.

Free of the bloodstained stones and the stacks of Temple
treasure,
Free of the bleating lambs and the bulls bellowing before
slaughter,
Free of the greediness of king and priest to take all we had,

From the smoking ruins of Jerusalem, the rabbis escaped
with us,
From the carcass of the lion of Judah
they taught us to bring forth sweetness.

> Rejoice, scholars and wise ones,
> Rejoice, teachers and masters,
> Rejoice, people of Israel.

And we built walls of inviolable custom around the Law,
and we inclosed the fresh springs of faith in tall dikes
until the water lay in stagnant pools.

Mourn for the Temple, but rejoice that it is gone;
Mourn for the walls that inclosed the Law,
and be glad they fell beneath the hammerblows of war.

Rejoice, Jews of Israel and Jews of the world,
Rejoice in the gift God gave our generation in agony:
Freedom to seek God alone, anew, to seek the Holy
One for ourselves.

Jews Confront History

Jacob

To cross the river into the land of Canaan,
Jacob had to wrestle with a stranger all night.

He had to struggle with some unknown being,
Perhaps the spirit of the river, or the guardian
of the land he sought to enter.

And as dawn broke he demanded and received
a blessing from the nameless one.

So it has often been for the Jew in history,
Beginning with Abraham and Sarah.

The Canaanites

When we entered into the land of Canaan,
we struggled with the people there,
taking the blessing of their language,
their myths and their poetry.

Our ancestors retold the stories of Eden,
of the flood, of the Tower of Babel,

Replacing the old, capricious, quarrelsome gods
with the One Lord of the World,
Who is just and peace-loving.

The Greeks

Wrestling with the Hellenistic peoples,
struggling to cross the boundaries into their culture,

The Pharisees and rabbis, Philo and even Josephus
led the way for us to learn new ways
and yet to retain the sacred core of Judaism.

We learned philosophy from them, and many new words:
"Synagogue" is a Greek word,
and "gematria," our version of geometry.

During Hellenistic times, with patience
and with logic they learned from the Greeks,
Our rabbis wrote the Mishna to guide us.

Islam

The great encounter of Israel and Islam
began in Arabia, but went forward to Spain.

Again Jews became wrestlers, our new Jacobs—
Judah Halevi, Moses Maimonides, Joseph Karo . . .

They learned grammar and poetry, science and medicine,
astronomy and astrology.

They learned, and they remained Jews, scholars,
faithful believers in one God, guardians of Torah.

The Italian Renaissance

In Italy, during the Renaissance,
there was a Jewish court musician, Solomon Rossi,
and a Jewish dancing master, William the Hebrew.

There was an opening to the world of the arts,
and a closing of the ghetto gates around the Jews.

In this volatile time, Simon Luzzatto led the Jews of Venice;
Soncino began to print Jewish books,
and a new age of learning opened before us.

Russia and Poland

Yet in the East, in Poland and Russia,
a different struggle went on between the Jews and their
    neighbors.

The Baal Shem Tov came forward, a new Jacob,
wrestling to demand a blessing of the Russian spirit,

Bringing joy to the Jewish peasants
and the promise of holy men, of *zaddikim*, to lead them.

Accepting the poverty of shtetl life,
they sought ecstasy rather than scholarship.

The Enlightenment

The wrestling and the struggles are not over.
Now all of us, in Europe, in America, in Israel
confront the Enlightenment.

For two hundred years it has engaged us,
first giving us the blessings of secular learning,
of citizenship and freedom, ours
with the help of Moses Mendelssohn.

Soon came the curse of anti-Semitism,
and Herzl led us toward political Zionism.

We burst into literature, science, and art,
suddenly proud of Heine, Disraeli, Marx,
Freud, Chagall, Einstein . . . and many more . . .

Then we confronted
the incomprehensible curse of the Holocaust.
And the unexpected blessing of an independent Israel.

New Jacobs arise for us in every generation:
Leo Baeck and Martin Buber,

Solomon Schechter and Mordecai Kaplan,
Abraham Heschel and Elie Wiesel . . .

Over and over again we have been injured
(as Jacob was injured)
but we have wrested our blessing from every new encounter.

We will continue our struggle with the West,
resisting its curses,
taking its blessings,
always preserving the deep center of Judaism.

Dedication of a New Torah

Our Torah is the great symbol of Jewish life today,
as it has been for more than two thousand years.

At first there was the menorah, the ark of the Covenant,
and then the Temple.

But before the Second Temple was built, the reading of
   Torah
became the great symbolic act of Jewish unity.

Medieval Jews honored the Torah with a rich cover and a
   crown,
as they had learned to honor royalty.

Modern Jews, like our ancestors,
stand in its presence and treat it with awe, a holy object.

It is a Tree of Life, we say,
therefore identifying it with the seven-branched menorah
that stood in the tabernacle and the Temple.

It contains the Law of Moses, we say,
identifying it with the Tablets of the Covenant
given on Mount Sinai.

Torah is the life and the length of our days, we say,
identifying it with the Temple, the center of Jewish life
in the past, and proclaiming it the center of Jewish life today
for ourselves and our people.

We stand in awe of these scrolls,
for they have preserved us as we have preserved them.
They are potent and they are dangerous:

Dangerous if we treat them like icons,
keep the scrolls rolled and look at the jeweled embroidery,
kiss the mantle and forget the words,

Dangerous even if we read the words and accept them as
    written
without understanding, without interpretation, without love.

Potent to make us seek eternal values in our temporary
    lives;
potent to set our minds and souls on the search for God.

This is our Torah. In it is the God-seeking of our people.
Let us use it with wisdom.

A Prayer for the Captives

To Israel and to the rabbis
and to the disciples and to all their disciples,
To all who study Torah in this place and in every place,
to them and to us,
Peace!

To Israel and to all those who are held captive,
to all those who are bound, accused, and tried,
who are imprisoned and kept in exile,
to them and to us,
Peace!

To Israel and to all those who will ransom the captive,
deliver the imprisoned, bring home the exile,
to those who will redeem the persecuted,
to them and to us,
Courage and strength!

To Israel and to Russia and to America,
to them and to us, be abundant peace,
freedom, courage, strength, grace, lovingkindness, mercy,
and salvation from our Father Who is in Heaven;
and let us say: Amen.

The Proud Worm

We people of the twentieth century are proud;
we have wiped out diseases, built great cities, traveled to
   the moon.

But if we cannot make peace, we may be once again
sick, hungry, wild creatures, if we survive at all.

God once spoke to our ancestor, saying:
"Fear not, you worm, Jacob, I will help you."*

We, too, are worms, and could become like worms,
crawling on the earth, dying like worms . . .

Peace is a new way of thinking,
a new way of relating to other nations,
new ways of behaving.

We who are half worm and half angel, being human,
must not cease our struggle to create peace.

God, we pray to You to help us make this quantum leap
into the next period of history,
the period of human peace.

*Isaiah 41:14

"The Heavens Declare the Glory of God"

PSALM 19

God wrote a record in rocks and stars,
The tale of creation for us to read.

The old earth, rivered with ice and molten rock,
Revolved through eons of thrusting mountains and grinding
glaciers.

The earth, first burning, then flooded and freezing,
Prepared through unhuman time the crust that would support
life.

God writes in the planets and galaxies and systems of stars
A continuing record of the universe.

God writes in vast symbols a story of unending creation
Of a universe expanding and bursting into outer space.

Trembling, we contemplate the work of God.
Trembling, we pray to our Creator:

You Who alone understand the world You are making.
Pity the weakness of our insights;

Forgive our faltering pursuit of knowledge;
Plant in us the drive to search for truth,

Add to our understanding the dimension of humility,
Teach us Your ways.

Ruaḥ

EZEKIEL 37:9

*Come, O breath, from the four winds, and breathe into
these slain that they may live again.*

And after the ghettoes and the camps
(The wind blew away the smoke and the ashes,
all that remained was a pile of shoes),

And after the White Papers closing the gates
(the sea carried away the bodies of the drowned),

And after exiles and wars and terrors,
When the Jewish people was surely slain,

A new wind blew into us,
and the sea washed to shore a bottle
with a note addressed to us, saying "Live!"

And the Israelis opened the gates
to Jews from every land,
And those in America rose up to help them.

And the young said, "Teach us, that we may be good Jews!"
And the women said, "Count on us, for we ARE Jews!"

And when they found the scrolls in the rubble of Europe
they sent them to synagogues (not to museums)
and in fear and trembling, Jews chanted their messages.

There were feet to walk in the way of the shoes,
And there were minds and hearts pledged
to redeem the life of the Jewish people,

For the wind that had blown away the smoke from the
   chimneys
returned with the divine spirit,
giving us a new birth in our day.
Hallelujah.

Elijah

MALACHI 3:23

Elijah the prophet, Elijah the Tishbite,
Elijah the forerunner of the Messiah,
long have we waited for you,
many times have we told tales of you:

You are an angel. With four beats
of your great wings you traverse the earth.

In a single night you built a palace
with many towers, and you disappeared
before the morning.

You have prolonged the life of the righteous;
you have turned away the angel of death
from the pious.

Now you sit in the heaven of heavens
and comfort the weeping Messiah;
you draw his head to your breast,
and still he weeps.

Elijah, the prophet, Elijah, the Tishbite,
Elijah, the forerunner of the Messiah,
for many generations we have not seen you.

We have learned to fly on wings of metal,
and we can build towers of glass in a night.

We turn away the demons of disease,
and keep even the angel of death
waiting in hospital corridors.

Yet still the Messiah weeps,
and he needs you to comfort him.

The proud and the wicked rule the earth;
in burning furnaces they prepare the day
of destruction, and who shall survive?

The Messiah who would redeem us
weeps, impotent and imprisoned,
in our hearts.

Comfort him, Elijah, strengthen him, Elijah,
and bring him forth at last!

Section Five
Almonds and Raisins

A Poem

With words
I must make a poem
a vine that grows,
blossoms, and bears fruit,
With words I must press the grapes,
make the wine,
and create the sensation
as it flows down your throat.

Ballad for Howard

Touching with stillness man and beast
White-hooded guest at the wedding feast,
Colder than ice, impartial as snow.
Sing him a song that all men know:
Song for the season of snow and ice,
    Love is the prize and death is the price.

Green grows the grass at the gatehouse door,
White blossoms cover the forest floor,
Bird songs begin before the morning,
Lover beware, remember, take warning:
When the blood runs, when the saps rise,
    Death is the price and love is the prize.

This is the song for mortal breath:
The prize is love, the price is death.
The prize is good, the price is great,
Green grows the grass at the garden gate.
Come walk with me, my love, today:
    We'll take our prize before we pay.

Farewell

In falling snow, I say farewell.
The cold flakes fall upon my lips —
No more remains for me to tell.

The cold flakes fall upon my lips
and stop the kiss that waited there.
I touch your mittened fingertips.

No more remains for me to tell,
Nor do you speak, but snowy stare
And though my heart will yet rebel

In falling snow I say farewell.
I could renounce you with such ease
if snow were pall, if breath would freeze.

For My Mother

Deep is the spring in wood and field,
The grass is rich and thick and deep,
The grain proclaims its promised yield,
In waves of green the green fires creep,
The fires of spring that spread and glow
And cover all the earth, and grow.

Mindless, the waxy leaves uncurl,
Heartless, your garden comes to bloom—
Tulips, scarlet and white, unfurl
Without recall or thought or gloom,
But you have gone from life and spring,
You cannot see nor work nor sing.

Now grief enlarges like a tree
And branches into every hour,
Heavy and green, grief grows in me,
Deepens its roots, bursts into flower,
Spreads like the green fires of spring,
And I am soil for this burning thing.

I stand to recite the proper prayer
"Extolled and magnified is the Lord,"
But you mock me on the empty air,
Though you cannot hear nor speak a word,
You cannot knit, your hands are still,
Yet I know your strength, your mind, your will.

Why did you go when warmth was in the air
Before you saw your trillium once again?
The grief for my father is old and rare
But now for you I grieve as I began,
Torn from you, weeping, with sobbing breath,
In the bitter green season of your death.

Not the Last Poem for Betty

I loved you because we were both grotesque,
You loved me because we were both beautiful.

The quality of your love haunts me
Despite the years since your death,
A death that had the same irony
As your clear sharp mind in your flabby body.

Though I have not found the truth in death,
I can see you smiling at the irony
While you hold your cigarette like a bum
Drawing in the last possible puff.

You have answered your own death to me
For I write letters to your ghost;
You have answered what is grotesque in me
For I struggle to meet your demand for beauty.

You were a scientist, and so I write of rocks;
You loved me, and so I write of love.

Granite is made of feldspar, quartz and mica;
Green malachite is a kind of copper ore;
But some rocks contain so many elements
Cemented together by pressure and heat
They are called conglomerate.

Few people are as good as granite for building
Or as beautiful as malachite for jewels;
But split on the cutting wheel of life
And polished with a rag of love,
Unexpected elements glow in the conglomerate.

I cannot pray to be made of something pure
For my identity is conglomerate;

But I can pray the sharp whirring wheels
Will cut through to something you saw
As lovely as malachite or as good as granite.

I can be thankful for your spirit,
I can pray you found the truth you sought,
I can wonder if immortality
Is a glow rubbed up by a rag of love.

Directions

"Turn me to You," I read, facing the orient,
Jerusalem, the holy city that like a magnet
draws our hearts. I face east, obedient,
to pray, though I have walked, wondering and mute,
in that divided city.

                           I seek direction.
I know this about polar expeditions:
Though you turn your head, standing at the south pole,
you would invariably face north. The conditions
of cold, exposure, even fear, might seem trivial
to someone who knows so certainly which way is north.
But where can we stand now, certain to know Your will,
to face toward You? Are there any polar places,
near or remote? Are there holy cities still?
God, overlook my weaknesses, my fears,
Turn me, I pray stubbornly: send me there.

The St. Croix River

Submerged in the orange murky water,
I long to float like fish forever,
but my body convulses to rise and fill with air.

They yank me into the boat, start the motor
and we bounce over the bumpy waves
propelled by explosions in the engine,
thrust forward at threatening speed.

The towering clouds, the solid glacial hills,
the wide river are foreign to us;
we live in the flying spray,
the foam of the wake,
the dying exhaust fumes.

Sun

Astronomers write in books
how distant you are in light-years,
how much bigger you are than earth,
Yet seen through my eyelashes,
as I lie on the grass, you make jumping bars
of rainbows, revolving circles of light.
Great sun, how can you be caught and refracted
in the slit of my nearly closed eye?

Building

Out of the cedars of the forests
the ores of the mountains
the stones of the hills
the copper of the desert,
from the earth itself,
the metals hidden in the earth
and the life that springs from the earth,
they built the Temple
where they came to worship
the Creator of the earth.
The Temple was a psalm of stone.

Icicle

Great solid icicles hang from the roof, shining in the sun.
Water flows through them, dripping from their fingers,
dropping into the snow, sinking, flowing, running,
down to the river where it is sucked up again
by the shining sun into the clouds, cooled
into snow, drops, freezes, melts, flows . . .
I love the bright solid form, the
free gift of icicles that
melt when I touch them.
Spirit is everywhere,
flowing, falling,
rising invisible
or as solid
as icicles
that melt
if you
touch
them.

Geese

Overhead we heard the quavering cries of wild geese
and saw them fly their giant arrow through the air.
"They complain so, and give their leaders no peace,"
I said, "They've got the whole sky. Don't they care?"
"That's no complaint, that cry is their radar,"
My friend laughs at me, "they listen to each other
flying blind through clouds. You've made our
world theirs. They've no leaders to complain to;
they shift. No bird can fly that arrowpoint for long."

"Gray birds, gray sky, and snow coming,"
I said, "somewhere in it there's a somber song."
"Laws of nature," snapped my friend, "and cold numbing
my hands. I'm going back now."
But I stood where snow met sky, gray as stone,
Who is there to head our arrow, cold, alone?

Winter

Falling, deeply fallen; the snow
continuous, silent, covers the ground
the roots of plants and trees, seeds, spores
cocoons, the various multitude of living cells,
covers completely, persistently
the white face of earth,
spreading relentlessly,
continuously,
as we who are masking, always masking,
deeply masking ourselves.

Sonnet for a Desperate Soul

I saw a trout that swam a sluggish pool
With slow and easy motion in brown reeds.
Supporting her was water viscous, cool,
The world in which she swims and fights and feeds.
Upward she flung herself with mighty leap,
Danced silver in the bright and alien air,
Fell back as from a mountain far too steep,
To pool and rest and comfort waiting there.
What could she see flipping through air and sun?
Did she feel free, or merely out of breath?
No doubt she told her mate what she had done
To dare the element that threatens death.
Yet who would count the ones who leap from pools
Of their own worlds to light and freedom, fools?

Wind Song

How shall I tame the wind?
With sails and rudder.
How shall I tame the wild waters?
With keel and rib.
Then shall I shout, Come wind,
Carry me far!
How shall I tame my heart?
With deeds of love.
How shall I tame my soul?
Only with prayer.

Now let me shout to You, my God,
as I shout to the wind,
Come!
I have prepared my heart for You
and my soul waits like an empty sail.
Surely You know how I have patched
the cracked hull, spliced the ravelled sheets. . . .
Come to me, God,
Come as the wind comes singing
in the rigging of the tall white ships.

Strange Bird

I woke at night and heard the falling rain,
The heavy raindrops rustled in the leaves
And softly dropped and pattered to the ground;
I woke because a strange bird sang,
Called out that night while all the others slept,
Listed with pride the things that it possessed,
"New mate, snug nest, sweet babes," it chirped and trilled.

I lay in darkness, heard the bright cries fade,
And thought how often I had echoed them,
Had told to all my pride in what I owned,
Announced possessions large and fine; and yet
A bird may have a nest, but for me
One thing is all I have: knowledge of death,
And that surrounds me like the dark of night,
And all I have or think I am will melt,
Drop, trickle, flow into a great river,
A river I could never map nor measure,
A river changing and shifting and moving forever.
Strange bird, sing out this summer night
But sing of a river whose waters fall
From evening skies or rise from springs in earth,
Sing of a river that no one can call "my own."

Sing of my single wealth: the knowledge of death
For this estate can open the soul to God,
Whose praises I can sing, like you, strange bird.
God sets the very bed where flows the stream,
And owns, creates and measures the vast waters,
God is in the springs of love,
The incessant rains of time,
the deep and holy river of life.

Though April

FOR MY MOTHER

Though April is the month to rise, still you,
Unrisen, deepen in the earth and me,
Sink deep, yet day by day I can't subdue
The tongues that lick and lick your memory
Until it melts and hardens and deceives.
I'll go to woods so deep the spring comes late,
Where trillium bloom, where heart believes,
Because you loved the wood, you will await
My voice. I'll walk and speak your name. In fall
I'll go again, when rain and leaves come down,
When vibrant in my ears, the shofar call
Shrieks for return, when mushrooms cluster brown.
When will you rise, return, and speak to me?
Where will I find your green and fragrant tree?

The Chagall Windows in Jerusalem

White light coming through stained glass
turns red, blue, glowing yellow, green,
shatters like light through a jewel
Into myriad colors, shimmering.

The meaning of light lies beyond us;
the qualities of light elude the theories:
waves that bend in water, particles, patterns,
none of these explain vision.

Look out your window at stars,
ponder the unsurpassable speed of light;
Look out your window at the Jews,
restless, searching in the moonlight.

They are the Jews you marched with in the wilderness,
you in your tribe, they in theirs,
twelve tribes of us marching in the wilderness,
with one ark, one Moses, one burning light ahead.

Now we are Israel, scattered through the nations,
shattered into many colors like the light,
eluding theories, marching through the world
with our vision before us.

Deep is the mystery of vision: ponder it.
Brilliant is the light of heaven: see in it.
Step through your window, search for your people,
Dwell among them, looking to their holy light.

On Cedar Lake, 1957

Before our skates had touched the pond that day
We knelt to see, imbedded in the ice,
A fish long dead, his frozen eye turned up;
And further on through surface clear and green
A sluggish waving weed in silent water.
But who might care for all that moves below?
Our skates are sharp, the air is bright,
The lake is wide; we swoop, we glide,
Take flight and dip and swerve
Like gulls. We fly, we fly.

A Riddle

The storyteller is asking riddles:
"How is an egg like a cloud?

"How is a match like a grain of wheat?
How is a pine cone like a word?"

The children try to guess.
"There is only one answer," she says.

The children are silent.
The storyteller speaks again:

"An egg makes a bird, a cloud makes rain,
matches make fire and wheat makes bread,
but a pine cone? And a word?"

Now a little girl with black braids
holds up her hand; she nods to her.

"When God began making the world,"
she says, "He spoke a word."

The children laugh, "Beginnings,"
they chant. "Beginnings, beginnings,
they are all beginnings."

"Ah," says the storyteller,
"And once upon a time there were people
who didn't know how to make beginnings, or even
how to recognize them,

"But beginnings are everywhere,
on the ground in seeds, in the sky in clouds,
in your mind in ideas, in your hand in tools to work with,
in your heart—your feelings—
and in the word of God."

The children smile
as they settle down to listen.

The storyteller will tell a tale
of the people who learned how to recognize beginnings
and how to make them.

Discovery

No one ever told me the coming of the Messiah
Could be an inward thing;
No one ever told me a change of heart
Might be as quiet as new-fallen snow.

No one ever told me that redemption
Was as simple as springtime and as wonderful
As birds returning after a long winter,
Rose-breasted grosbeaks singing in the swaying branches
Of a newly budded tree.

No one ever told me that salvation
Might be like a fresh spring wind
Blowing away the dried withered leaves of another year,
Carrying the scent of flowers, the promise of fruition.

What I found for myself I try to tell you:
Redemption and salvation are very near,
And the taste of them is in the world
That God created and laid before us.   '

Boiling Springs

Water is essential to life everywhere, but nowhere more than in the desert. When Isaiah calls, "All who are thirsty, come and drink," he is speaking of faith in a metaphor of great meaning to a desert people. "Boiling Springs" is a real place in Minnesota.

The rain falls in summer on my green hill.
It trickles through layers of soil and sand
Through caverns and rocks below the land
To rivers unknown, in darkness and chill.

The waters above meet the waters below
Rushing unheard through the caverns of stone
Dropping and flowing in places unknown
Except for one pond, one spring that I know.

There at the foot of the quiet green hills
The waters boil up in the light of day
And run to the river a few miles away
To float the barges and power the mills.

I look at the pond which is never the same.
The waters were low some years, some high;
But my spring bubbled on, it never went dry,
The water was there whenever I came.

These waters will rise through soil and shale
Though the hills are brown and the grass dried hay.
Though the sun burn the earth day after day,
I believe: these waters will never fail.

For My Daughter

The children are playing
By the river in the snow
Down beside the water
Where the willows grow.
Like a willow is my daughter
Supple and straight
Like a willow by the water
When spring is late.
In all the wood and meadow
The only sign of spring
Is the willow turning yellow
With her welcoming.
Your joys root deep, my daughter.
Your sorrows shallow,
Learn from willows by the water–
Life is to hallow.

Verse for a Mystic

These are some things that sailors know:
Though the air be quiet, though the west wind blow,
Tied to their moorings or set adrift,
Rigged with white sails or tall masts bare,
Ships swing and slip, they turn and shift,
And they face the wind, be it foul or fair.

These are some things that sailors know:
Though the air be quiet, though a stiff wind blow,
They can tack to starboard, they can tack to port,
They can haul in and point, or take a broad reach,
Cleat down the sheets and high-side for sport
Or run downwind toward a waiting beach.

There is only one way that they cannot go:
Toward the heart of the wind, the source of the blow.
For if they do, the sails will fall slack,
The tiller will swing, the boat lie still,
They must struggle to find a better tack
So the hull will plane, so the sails will fill.

This is a thing that sailors know:
Though the south breeze play, though the north wind blow,
The wind can take you across the seas,
But if you come close, too close to the source,
You will stand as still as the landlocked trees.
Good sailors keep to their charted course.

Ships and boats want to face their master,
Are content to lie at their moorings in peace,
But sailors forever want to sail faster
With spray in their faces their speed increase,
Their spinnakers fill when the light winds blow;
Toward the source of power they do not go.

The Odyssey and the Exodus

Ulysses sailed the wine-dark sea;
Moses paced the burning sands of Sinai.

Despite the tricks of his gods on Olympus,
Bravely Ulysses searched his way home;

With fire by day and smoke by night,
Steadfastly the God of Moses led him forward.

Ulysses traveled by his wits and his courage;
Moses walked according to God's word.

When Ulysses at last reached home
He brought news of the victory at Troy;

When the people of Moses reached the Promised Land
They carried with them the tables of the Law.

Plato, a descendant of Ulysses,
Taught that God was a perfect idea;

Isaiah, descendant of Moses, found God in human history,
The moral demand in the lives of human beings.

The Greeks said, "Man is the measure of all things,"
And "For a full life, practice moderation;"

"God measures man!" shouted the prophets,
And the Jews practiced Kiddush ha-Shem. *

Now Greek and Jew alike sail oceans dark with danger,
All nations wander deserts parched with peril;

All yearn for the homes of their youth,
All long for a promised land of peace.

We pray to the one God of us all
For the courage of the Greeks and the passion of the
    prophets.

*"Sanctification of the name" (of God) i.e., martyrdom   210

For the great qualities of all the peoples of the earth,
For everything we need for the journey God has commanded
   us to make.

Let us go forward, God, in our time,
On the journey which will bring peace to us all.

Syllogism

All men are mortal, and Socrates was a man
Therefore he took the hemlock, brave Athenian.

Socrates' "therefore" was taught to all mankind
It held the seed of knowledge, the genesis of mind.

All of us are mortal, and Moses was a man
But was the gift of life forever under ban?

"I set before You here this day a choice;
Therefore choose life," thundered the Voice.

Divine, that "therefore" burned, hotter than Pharaoh's coal,
Fired Moses with power to lead, and brought the birth of soul.

Count one wise who has mastered the logic of Socrates
And blessed who learns to love the law of Moses,

Count as human, mortal, blessed and wise
One whose mind and soul make Moses' choice before he
    dies.

The Doe

Like a dappled deer quietly
Lying in the dappled shade
Of a great oak in the king's park,
A deer whose ear twitches at sounds
A little like the hunter's horn,
Whose shank trembles at the remembered pain
Of the iron spikes surrounding the park,
I wait in stillness
Trembling, remembering,
Listening for the hunter.
Who is the hunter?
He is the king.
What does he want of me?
Only pain.
At the edge of the dark wood
Beyond the iron spikes,
Standing in shadows,
Her shawl wrapped about her,
Waits the dark mother
Whom I long to embrace.
Who is the dark mother?
She is death.
What will she give me?
Her cold peace.

On First Looking into My Son's Chemistry Book: O

Nobody can see you, hear you, taste, touch, or smell you,
Yet you are essential to life,
being part of air and water,
not to mention rust, tarnish, and flame,
deluge and conflagration.
Who do you think you are,
God or somebody?

Returning to Jerusalem, 1957

Though you have never entered Jerusalem before
You who enter the holy city, return;
Return to cross a small stony valley, empty in the afternoon
    sun,
And to climb a stony hill where goats graze on wild poppies.

Standing among the ancient buildings on the hill
You mutter a quick prayer, and your feet kick a stone
That masons may have placed in the tomb of David. Then
Under the chrome-hot sky, sweating in the desert wind,
You climb down the hill of Zion and cross the Valley of
    Gehenna
To reach again human dwelling places.

City of Gehenna, no traveler is a stranger to you,
For in your small stony valley, where snipers sometimes hide,
Living infants were thrown in the fires of Moloch;
Battles for Jerusalem have raged there, men killing
With sword and crossbow, arquebus and rifle,
Molotov cocktail and tommy gun.

City of Zion, no traveler can be a stranger to you,
For on Mount Zion Jeremiah wept and shouted at the king,
And on Mount Zion Isaiah saw his vision, three times holy,
And dreamed of peace among all the creatures of the earth;
And from Mount Zion, the traveler prays,
The Law will at last go forth to all the nations.

Traveler to Jerusalem, a bulldozer could level that mountain
With its impossible dreams, and fill in that valley of death,
For the moments of vision on the hill are hardly worth
The dying screams of the infants or the agonies of the young
    soldiers.

City of all we dread and all we dream, Jerusalem,
Holy city, let them tear down your mountain and fill up your
    pit!

But glorious in the setting sun, with every pink stone house
    aflame with light,
Jerusalem stands, solid for centuries past and centuries to
    come.
It is the horror of Gehenna and the hope of Zion
Built in our souls as solid as this city
That make of every one of us
Travelers returning to Jerusalem,
Holy city . . . human city.

Safed

They built above the clouds who built Safed,
Cobbled her crooked streets around the mountaintop,
Dug her stone stairs into the steepest slopes,
Leaned her houses against the mountainside;
Below them, through the mists, sparkled the Sea of Galilee,
And above them, the open sky.

Descending the grooved steps is a woman of Safed
Carrying a great jar of water on her head;
She passes a robed and bearded man, a goat
Grazing on a rooftop, a loaded donkey;
She hears the thin chant of the men
In the ancient house of study;

As she enters the stone arch of her home
Bearing her jar of water for her children,
She passes the walled courtyard of the artist
Who once painted the lost village of his youth
But now paints his spreading figtree and the curling tendrils of
    his vine.

I pray for anyone in any place not Safed
Who builds or paints or studies,
I pray for anyone who everywhere bears the waterjar,
I pray that every one may find a way
To dwell in a timeless city above the clouds.

My Daughter, My Son

My Daughter
Chattering, she pulls dresses off hangers,
drops them in the trunk with the books and papers,
hugs me quickly as she bumps past,
while I stand there talking, advising,
reminding, full of such wisdom. . . .
But I was always the one who packed
and went away to college.
How did this become, that she is I
and I am Mother?

      My Son
      You are simply surprised
      at the red streak on your wrist,
      annoyed at me with the hot wet towels.
      making you sit still so long.
      You never watched the stopping of breath,
      felt the last delicate flutter of a heart.
      Yet even as I fuss and scold
      I believe that in you
      is the tender thrust of the seedling
      that cracks the rock.

Saturday Morning
in the Country of Old Men:
The Smoky Mountains in October

The trees have been driven
from the valleys and the meadows,
they have retreated to the rocky mountainside.
The creek, mourning its sources,
murmuring that it will lose itself
in the river and the ocean,
cries continuously as I climb.

Mostly the trees are old,
and the young birches grow from aching, mossy stumps.
I see an oak split lengthwise years ago by lightning,
a sweetgum fighting red among the bare, defeated poplars,
a chestnut, stripped of its bark,
dead of fungus, but erect.

The trail turns along a ledge of limestone
to a high place of stunted, wind-bowed pines.
The mountain peaks retreat into mist.
In the guidebook,
I find no names for them.

Names? I need no map.
I know this hour. I know it well.
It is Saturday morning in the country of the old men.
On that day, the old men, old as the trees,
twisted, defeated, driven, enduring as the trees,
mumble their mourning, their remembering, regretting,
murmur continuously as the falling creek . . .

No stranger to this hour
I turn away, letting my legs
go running down the hills,
hurrying to leave behind
the murmuring voices,
the high, broken incessant voices,
rushing away from the old men
and the place of vision.

For Nelly Sachs

Driving through fall
The car incloses me.
Like a stone image
I sit, foot on gas pedal,
responding only to traffic signs.

If the leaves crunch under my tires,
I don't hear them;
if the butterflies blown against the radiator
crumble to dust and fall away,
I haven't touched them.

All that I notice of fall
is sunlight
filtering through the smoke of burning leaves;
if it grows cold,
I will turn on the heater.

Would it matter if a stone image
crumbled to dust
or went up in smoke?
Could I get out of this car
and walk again?

The Wall: The Poem I Couldn't Write

When we went to Israel in October, 1967, I had an experience that has always stayed with me. I wanted to write a poem about it, but I never could. I was ready and eager to go to the Western Wall, to share the great religious experience that many, like Heschel, had spoken and written about, Jerusalem reunited! The wall, the Western wailing wall, the last bit of the holy temple, is ours now!

We walked in mobs through the shuk on David Street, feeling for the grooved steps, going down, down . . . too many people to be able to see our feet as we walked, finally coming to a clearing. There, across an open paved area, was the wall, as I had seen it in pictures, with tufts of green in the cracks of the great stones. I hurried toward it . . .

And an Israeli soldier stopped me, grabbed my arm roughly, shoved me to one side. With total unbelief, I realized that women, Jewish women, could not approach the wall in the place so often pictured in books and displayed in synagogues, so often pictured that it lived in my mind. Women must go to the right, to a small separate place. I was hurt and bewildered. This area was outdoors, not a synagogue, and the old pictures from pre-state times had shown men and women together, praying at the wall. Seldom have I felt so rejected by my own people as I did then. Seldom have I felt so alien as when I approached the women's area and saw old women pushing bits of paper with their prayers written on them into the chinks in the wall. I had seen the Indians in the Mexican cathedrals leaving bits of paper to pray for health or rain or babies or to thank the saints for favors received. Is this Judaism? Can an educated woman be a Jew? Can any woman be a Jew? In that hour I became a Jewish feminist.

My Talit

FOR MY HUSBAND

You took me to your synagogue
for the first time on Yom Kippur, 1941.

Everything was white: the Torah mantles,
the rabbi's robes, the flowers.

White light fell on the white heads
and white shawl-covered shoulders of the men.

Everything was white
except for the dark dresses and black hats
we women were wearing.

Years passed like white clouds,
changing shape, drifting by, until 1982.

You made me a talit,
you tied the knots, put it on my shoulders,
kissed me.

Now when we go to our synagogue
I am part of the whiteness,
part of the silent prayer for purity.

The River

The golden leaves are falling, falling in the sunlight.
The migrant birds are crying in the emptied trees.
The moving waters glisten, glimmer in the sunlight,
Moving, changing, flowing as if they'd never freeze.

Who can know the river, the unknown river?
Buoys and charts are words on the river of the mind,
And a poem is a crystal, ice from the river,
Formed when the yearning of the heart is defined.

The golden rhymes are falling, falling in the river.
The meters and the rhythms are sinking out of sight.
The word of God is forming, freezing on the river.
I reach and try to grasp it, but I break it in my fright.

Grandmother

Rocking gently in her chair
the grandmother holds the new baby,
cuddling him in the crook of her arm.

His little body is soft, warm, and fragrant;
his round eyes open, gazing into hers.
His tiny fist curls around her finger.

Down the years, she knows
his eyes will look at sights
she will not live to see.

She knows his hands will reach out
to grasp the hands of friends
unknown to her.

His tiny feet will grow to walk in new paths,
His heart will lead him where he will.

Knowing all this, she has no fear,
for God is with her.

She rocks the baby and her love enfolds him.
His eyes close and he sleeps.

Sensing God's presence supporting her, she smiles,
knowing she holds a whole world in her hands.

Only the Young

Grief taints my ripening peach, guilt browns my pear,
Experience reveals some blemish everywhere.
Only the young taste pleasures ripe and whole.
For perfect joy, long life disqualifies the soul.

Power Saws

In the summer
the saws were buzzing and whining everywhere,
streets blocked by sawyers cutting up elms,
and everywhere the marks on diseased trees
foretold the coming of destruction,
the felling of the giants. . . .
In the summer
my friends were falling like trees.

But in the fall
where the elms left bare sky and bald houses,
men came with mechanical shovels
and truckloads of small trees
to plant in the round holes.
Now I drive by rows of young maples,
waving their red mittens
in greeting and farewell,
like grandchildren.

Private Ritual: A Ḥasidic Tale Retold

The place was a wood in Wisconsin,
The people were my mother, my father, my brothers and
    myself,
The time was after Yom Kippur.
The ritual was to cut branches of bittersweet,
tie them with string, hang them upside down
to wait for the orange berries to pop open, showing the
    red inside,
to admire them all winter for their beauty.

We cannot return to the wood: houses have been built
    there.
We cannot go with the same people,
my mother, my father and one of my brothers have died.
But Yom Kippur still comes
And we can find bittersweet, even if we must buy it,
We can be thankful for the bright red berries in the window
when the white snow covers all the colors of the earth.

Music

The music begins, sparkles like diamonds,
shattering into brilliant colors,
brightens the listener's faces,
drives the musicians to play harder,
to sing higher . . .

My son is a musician, a magician of sound,
a master who gathers sound like light,
whose music fills the room with jewels of tone,
whose magic divides the light
into sapphires, emeralds, topaz, rubies
dancing in rhythm on rays of light,
rising in the shimmering air,
visions of ascending worlds.

When Death Comes

When death comes to the person you love
you will go down to darkness and despair
and in the depths of loneliness will find
your naked soul, craven and cold.

You whose mind has considered and doubted,
whose heart has faltered, and whose courage has failed,
will wring out the final personal word
from your stricken soul.

And death has no truth but this: I believe.
Death has no victory but this:
to rise from doubt and cold darkness
to magnify and hallow the name of God.

The Pendulum

Like a pendulum I swing
from here, through center, to there,
my path three points on an arc:
detachment, loneliness, concern:
involvement, depression, detachment.
Centripetal my motion, centrifugal
I swing, suspended, vascillating,
dreading the motionless center,
moving, I think, through these:
engagement, discouragement, freedom;
freedom, isolation, engagement.

And yet when a pendulum swings
from here, through center, to there,
every point on the arc of its passage
remains an invariable distance
from its master, the clock. And I
swinging down, through center, and up,
Shall I ever approach or recede
from the point of my suspension?

Miami Beach

And do you know the land where orange trees bloom?
And have you seen the beaches in the sun,
The roads like ribbons from a golden loom,
Winding through orchards, crossing dunes, to run
Down to the towering city by the sea?
There people move as languorous as eels
With underwater ease. They gather free
The colored shells that wait along the shores
Or feast, or bathe, or wander on high heels
To buy the golden trinkets in the stores.

Oh yes, I know the land where orange trees bloom,
Where great hotels house worshippers of sun,
Preserve each person in a separate room,
The odd, the old, the lovers of their fun;
Each in a neon pyramid, with key
To his deposit box, and deck of cards
And dressing gown of silk, as regally
As Tut, embalms himself, a pharaoh
Counting all he owns, possesses, guards,
Although his door is closed, his bed is narrow.

Curaçao

In the oldest synagogue in the Western Hemisphere,
there is white sand on the floor,
the sand of God's promise to Abraham.
White sand
running through fingers
as it runs through an hour glass
measures ages of wandering from the womb of the desert
to this island in the sea.
White sand, fine and eternal,
like the people, easily scattered, hard to destroy,
clinging to the fingers of God.

Surgery

You go down into soft darkness,
down, down until
nothing . . .

The machine is gently breathing for you,
you sleep,
like grass seed, you can't see the sun,
but you know where it is.
You are deep in the darkness
of earth
but moving toward the light,
slowly you push up out of the darkness,
hear voices you know,
lift your eyelids,
see anxious faces—your family—
why are they worried
when you are so warm, sleepy, happy?
Dry mouth, ice chips on a wooden stick
sleep, sleep,
hands turn you in a warm nest
of pillows.

Coming up, coming up,
the tubes are gone from my mouth and throat,
breathing by myself,
I could speak,
but do I need to?

Another day, another room,
I'm waking up. I hear people around me,
slowly I open my eyes,
reach toward consciousness,
more aware than a blade of grass in the sun.

Up out of the dark place three times,
three times in seven years,
still myself, still alive.

I say: Thank you,
doctors, nurses, researchers,
Thank you, God.

General Index

Index of Biblical References